Decluttering and Downsizing the Family Home

Strategies for a Stress-Free Transition, Learn to Let Go of Clutter, Plan a Successful Move and Embrace a Fresh Start

I0161867

Rebecca Lawson

Table of Contents

Introduction

Sarah and Tom had spent over two decades in their spacious four-bedroom house, filled with fond memories of laughter, family gatherings, and the pitter-patter of their children's feet. But as life evolved, so did their needs.

Their children had grown up and moved away, leaving empty rooms that felt increasingly silent and lonely. The couple often found themselves overwhelmed by the responsibilities of maintaining such a large home. One day, after reflecting on their situation over coffee, they realized they wanted to embrace a simpler life, free from the clutter and upkeep that weighed them down.

They set off on the daunting task of sorting through their belongings, reminiscing about each item. Old toys, photo albums, and furniture evoked laughter and tears. Together, they decided what to keep and what to let go. They held a garage sale, inviting neighbors to take a piece of their history home.

Once their home was on the market, the couple found a charming little cottage on the outskirts of the city. It was cozy and had a beautiful garden—something they had always dreamed of. The move was bittersweet; they cherished the memories of their old home, but the promise of a new beginning was exciting.

As they settled into their new place, Sarah and Tom found joy in their newfound freedom. They spent weekends gardening, exploring nearby parks, and connecting with new neighbors. The downsizing journey transformed their lives, allowing them to focus on what truly mattered: celebrating life together. Through this experience, they learned that home isn't just a place, but a feeling—a feeling they carried with them in their hearts.

Life is an ever-flowing river, guiding us through twists and turns, sometimes gentle, sometimes turbulent. For those standing on the banks of midlife or beyond, one of these significant bends in the river may be the decision to downsize the family home. This is more than just a practical move; it is a journey that requires both courage and resilience. The mere thought of parting with a home filled with cherished memories and possessions can seem overwhelming, but amid this change lies an opportunity for renewal and liberation.

Downsizing is about making room for new experiences and embracing a lifestyle aligned with your current needs. The process presents unique challenges and rewards, offering a chance to reflect on what truly matters. It's about letting go while also holding on to the essence of what makes a house a home. Memories aren't tied to square footage, yet the shift can stir emotions that feel deeply connected to the walls you've lived within.

Leaving behind a home that has been the backdrop of countless life events can bring up waves of nostalgia and reluctance. These thoughts might make it tempting to cling to what's familiar. However, embracing the idea of downsizing means recognizing the freedom it can offer. Imagine fewer responsibilities and more time to explore your passions. Perhaps consider the benefits of living within a community designed for people who are at the same stage in life, where connection and shared experiences foster new friendships.

The fears you or your loved ones might experience at the prospect of leaving your much-loved family home are common. This is where this book comes in. Throughout 10 chapters and a conclusion, you will learn how to transition and embrace the new life as easily and stress-free as possible.

About This Book

The purpose of this book is to accompany you on this transformative path. It seeks to provide not only practical strategies but also compassionate advice as you navigate the intricacies of decluttering and transitioning to a new, smaller living space. It's a guide built on understanding the practical and emotional complexity of this task. In these pages, you'll find tools to break down the process into manageable steps, ensuring you don't feel lost along the way. From handling sentimental treasures to organizing logistics, we've got you covered.

This book provides a thoughtful exploration of the decluttering and downsizing process, starting from the initial planning stages through to establishing comfort and happiness in your new surroundings. We'll discuss how to prioritize belongings and make decisions about what to keep, discard, donate, or sell, all while keeping in mind the emotional weight these items carry. Furthermore, you'll learn how to tackle common hurdles that arise during such transitions without feeling overwhelmed.

Your new beginning awaits, a fresh chapter filled with limitless possibilities. Downsizing can lead to a life unencumbered by unnecessary clutter—physical and mental. It gives room for clarity and focuses on what truly adds value to your life. Whether it's more time for hobbies you love, increased financial flexibility, or simply a less demanding lifestyle, the benefits are yours to define and embrace.

Within these pages, you will find everything you need to transform this chapter of your life into something rewarding and joyful. Here's to finding new homes for old loves and creating new spaces for future joys. Enjoy the ride—you're in great company.

Chapter 1

Understanding the Need for Downsizing

Downsizing is a choice many people face at various stages of life, often provoking a blend of excitement and uncertainty. With life constantly evolving, the need to adjust our living spaces to better suit our circumstances becomes not just practical but necessary. Perhaps it's the kids heading off to college or retiring from decades of work, prompting a reflection on what truly matters in our homes. Here we explore why downsizing is such a common experience, and how it can be both an emotional and liberating journey. While the concept of moving into smaller spaces might seem overwhelming at first, it's a chance to declutter not just homes, but also minds, leading to more focused, time-rich living.

Below, we'll delve into the myriad reasons that drive individuals to consider downsizing. Join us as we unpack this significant life change, offering insights and guidance for those ready to embrace new possibilities.

Why Do People Downsize?

Downsizing is a decision often influenced by various factors, each carrying its own weight in the lives of those considering a change. Let's delve into these motivations and understand why downsizing becomes an appealing choice for many.

Aging

Aging often nudges people toward smaller, more manageable living arrangements. As you grow older, maintaining a larger home can become daunting. The upkeep of a big house often requires substantial energy and resources, which may no longer be readily available to older adults. By opting for a smaller space, you can conserve your energy for activities you enjoy or need, such as social engagements or passion projects. A smaller home also typically means fewer stairs, less cleaning, and reduced yard work, aligning well with the changing physical capabilities that accompany aging.

Life Transitions

Life transitions, such as children leaving home or retirement, significantly impact housing needs. The departure of grown children leaves many parents with more space than they need, prompting them to reassess their living situation. This stage, often called "empty nesting," allows parents to explore new housing options that better suit their lifestyle post-child-rearing. Similarly, retirement opens up opportunities to relocate to areas with climates or communities that match retirees' desired lifestyles. Many seek out smaller residences in vibrant neighborhoods, retirement communities, or even cities popular with active seniors. This shift not only reflects new life stages but also supports the pursuit of personal interests and hobbies without the burden of maintaining a large family home.

Financial Considerations

Financial considerations are often a key driving force behind the decision to downsize. With increasing costs of living and economic uncertainties, many see downsizing as a way to reduce expenses. Smaller homes not only come with lower mortgage payments but also decrease utility bills, property taxes, and maintenance costs. Additionally, selling a larger property to purchase a more modest home often frees up equity. This financial relief can be a prime motivator for downsizing, especially for retirees relying on fixed incomes or savings. These extra funds can be invested, used for travel, or to simply provide peace of mind for future financial security.

Lifestyle Changes

Lifestyle changes further motivate people to embrace downsizing. There is a growing trend toward minimalism and simplicity, where individuals choose to focus on experiences rather than possessions. A smaller home encourages decluttering and intentional living, helping individuals prioritize what truly matters to them. This shift can lead to a sense of freedom and empowerment, as letting go of excess belongings opens up possibilities for new adventures. Smaller homes often require less time for upkeep, allowing people to pursue passions like travel, hobbies, or volunteer work. This aligns with the modern desire for flexibility and adaptability, promoting a lifestyle that values quality of life over materialism.

Benefits of Downsizing

Embracing a smaller living space can offer significant benefits, especially for those considering downsizing during midlife or later stages. This was certainly the case for Clara:

Clara had lived in her spacious four-bedroom home for over 20 years. With her children grown and moved away, the house felt empty, and Clara found herself overwhelmed by the amount of stuff she had accumulated over the years. She often lamented how her once peaceful home had turned into a cluttered maze of boxes and unused furniture.

Eventually, Clara decided it was time to downsize. The thought of moving into a cozy two-bedroom apartment excited her, but she knew it meant she had to part with many cherished belongings. Initially, the idea of letting go was daunting. However, as she started sorting through her possessions, Clara rediscovered old memories—photos, letters, and keepsakes that brought her joy.

With each item she decided to let go, Clara felt a sense of relief. She made several trips to a local charity shop with bags of clothes she hadn't worn in years, toys her children had outgrown, and furniture that no longer fit her lifestyle. She also held a garage sale, not only clearing space but also connecting with neighbors, sharing stories, and creating a sense of community.

As moving day approached, Clara was amazed at how much freer she felt. With less stuff, she had more time and energy to focus on what truly mattered: her friendships, hobbies, and exploring the city she loved. In her new apartment, everything had its place, and she found herself enjoying a simpler, more organized life.

In the end, downsizing not only lightened Clara's physical load but also uplifted her spirit. She felt revitalized, embracing newfound freedom, and was able to create a home that reflected her current self—one filled with beauty, peace, and the joy of living in the moment. Downsizing was not just about the space; it was a journey of rediscovery and renewal.

Below, we look at some of the benefits associated with downsizing to a smaller property.

Embracing a Simpler Life

One of the most profound advantages of downsizing is the opportunity to simplify life through decluttering and focusing only on essential possessions. Imagine walking into your home and feeling a sense of calm rather than chaos. By letting go of items that no longer serve a purpose, you create a serene environment that increases overall well-being and mental clarity. This shift toward minimalism allows you to prioritize what truly matters and brings joy, making everyday living more intentional and rewarding.

Personal Growth and New Opportunities

Another fascinating aspect of downsizing is the potential for personal growth and new opportunities. Moving to a fresh environment often comes with an invigorating sense of rebirth. It's a chance to redefine how you wish to live your life and set new goals, both big and small. The process of finding and adapting to a new space can ignite creativity and foster resilience. You might discover new communities or activities that align with your evolving interests and desires, which can be incredibly fulfilling. Embracing change, even when it's challenging, can lead to unexpected adventures and enrich your life in ways you hadn't anticipated.

Deeper Appreciation for What You Have

Downsizing can contribute to a deeper appreciation of experiences over material goods. When your living area is limited, you become selective about what you bring into your home, ensuring that each piece serves a practical purpose or holds sentimental value. This mindfulness can transition into other aspects of life, encouraging more meaningful interactions and connections. Rather than accumulating needless possessions, you're more likely to spend time creating memories with loved ones or engaging in activities that you enjoy. This shift in focus from things to experiences can lead to a more enriched and intentional way of living.

Healthier Living

Downsizing often encourages a healthier lifestyle, as smaller spaces promote spending more time outdoors. With fewer rooms to maintain, you might find yourself spending more time in nature, whether it's enjoying a daily walk, exploring local parks, or visiting community centers. Moving to a smaller home closer to urban amenities or natural landscapes can spark a newfound zest for outdoor exploration and community involvement.

Common Challenges and Roadblocks

Downsizing can be a daunting experience, particularly if you have become emotionally attached to your home, as it was the setting of so many happy times. This sense of attachment can make it difficult to let go, turning the process into an emotional journey that requires careful preparation and support.

It's essential to acknowledge these emotions rather than suppress them. Many people find comfort in discussing their feelings with family members or friends who understand their history and attachment to their home. Support groups or speaking with downsizing specialists can also provide invaluable assistance in navigating these complex emotions.

Another obstacle in downsizing is the logistical challenge of determining what to keep, donate, discard, or sell. The sheer volume of accumulated possessions can be overwhelming, leading individuals to feel stuck or paralyzed by the decision-making process. Creating an inventory list can serve as a practical step forward. Begin by categorizing items according to their importance and frequency of use. Choosing one room at a time or starting with less emotionally significant areas can ease this process.

An inventory list can be fun. For instance, when Lucy suggested she and her husband, Tim, create an inventory list of their belongings, he proposed, "Let's make it interesting! For every item we list, we need to come up with a funny story about it!"

Excited by the challenge, they got to work. They started with the first item, a cactus Lucy had named Spike. Tim confidently proclaimed, "Spike here is our alarm clock! He once stabbed me in the foot when I forgot to water him for a week!" Lucy burst into laughter, remembering how Spike had survived a 10-day trip when they accidentally left him behind during a vacation.

Next on their list was a massive, inflatable unicorn, which they had bought for a pool party several summers ago. Tim grinned. "Ah, yes! We can't forget 'Uni'! He made quite the splash—literally. Remember when he popped during the party and left kids crying and running away?" They both doubled over in laughter, recalling the sight of soggy children trying to paddle away on half-deflated unicorn remains.

As they continued through their home, they stumbled across an extensive collection of mismatched socks in a drawer. With a raised eyebrow, Lucy asked, "What do we do about these?" Tim quickly replied, "Ah, 'The Lonely Sock Brigade,' an elite group of socks seeking their long-lost partners!" They both giggled as Lucy added, "Perhaps they'll find their soulmates in the laundry of the new house!"

With each item, their inventory list was filled with not only belongings but also their shared laughter and silly stories. It became an outrageous adventure, turning what could be a mundane task into an evening of joy.

Particularly valuable are the services offered by downsizing experts who can help streamline these tasks. They can assist not only in sorting belongings but also in organizing estate sales or organizing donations, thus lightening the load significantly. They can guide those involved through the selling process, ensuring that treasured items find new homes where they will be used and appreciated.

Resistance to change is a natural human response, especially when facing a massive upheaval. Embracing a gradual approach can soften this transition. Start by making small changes in daily routines that reflect the anticipated lifestyle shift. Visiting potential new living spaces regularly before moving can also help create familiarity, reducing anxiety about the unknown.

How to Prepare for Downsizing

Psychologically preparing for this change involves setting realistic goals and expectations. It is important to acknowledge that adapting takes time, and there might be moments of discomfort along the way. Below, we present some tips to help you prepare to downsize.

Have a Timeline

Whether you have a set date or have just made the decision to downsize, developing a comprehensive timeline can be beneficial, detailing each step from the initial stages of decluttering to settling into the new home. This detailed plan provides structure and a sense of control over the process.

To develop a timeline for moving house, follow these steps:

1. **Set a Moving Date**: Choose a specific date for your move.

2. **Create a Timeline**: Start from the moving date and work backward.

3. **Assign Tasks**: We present an example of what this might look like below. Remember, this will differ depending on the size of your house and the unique details of your move!

    o   8 weeks before: Begin decluttering and sorting items.

    o   6 weeks before: Start packing nonessential items.

    o   4 weeks before: Notify landlords, schools, and utilities about the move.

    o   2 weeks before: Confirm moving arrangements and pack essential items.

    o   1 week before: Finalize packing and clean the house.

    o   Moving day: Complete the move and conduct a final walk-through.

4. **Use a Planner**: Consider using digital tools or apps to manage tasks and deadlines.

5. **Stay Flexible**: Be prepared to adjust the timeline as needed.

By following these steps, you'll create a comprehensive timeline to ensure a smooth moving process. Remember, it generally takes longer than you think to move, so be kind to yourself along the way!

Include Family and Friends

Including family and friends in the downsizing can add a layer of emotional support and shared responsibility. They can offer objective perspectives, helping distinguish between genuinely needed items and those saved purely out of nostalgia. Inviting them to participate in sorting sessions may also lend some levity to the task and transform it into a bonding experience, rather than a solitary endeavor.

For instance, setting clear intentions early on can guide the entire transition process. Decide on what kind of living environment is most desirable in the long term, taking into account factors like location, size, and community amenities. Discussing these goals with loved ones ensures everyone is aligned and supportive of the decisions being made.

Document

Letting go of household items does not mean losing cherished memories. Consider documenting stories and anecdotes associated with particular objects, either through writing or creating digital photo albums. This allows you to preserve the essence of the past without needing the physical items to prompt memories. Passing down certain heirlooms to younger generations can ensure that family traditions continue and memories live on in loved ones.

Seek Professional Help

Consider seeking professional guidance not only for logistical support but also for practical tips on maintaining independence in a new living space. Professionals can offer insight into spatial organization, maximizing functionality in smaller residences, and connecting with community resources. This type of focused help enables individuals to adjust to their new surroundings while ensuring that their needs and preferences are honored in the new setting (What not to do when downsizing?, 2024).

Summary

Downsizing, as we've explored, is a multifaceted decision that has both practical and emotional dimensions. Whether driven by aging, financial necessity, or the desire for a simpler lifestyle, it will change your life. The journey of letting go of a family home or a house that has been host to many happy memories can be emotionally charged. Yet the gains are equally compelling; a smaller living space offers reduced maintenance and financial relief, freeing up time and resources to focus on what matters—personal growth, new experiences, and enriched interpersonal relationships. One of the aims of this book is to help you with that. In the following chapters, we will discuss many of the topics we have touched on here in detail, helping you make your big move that much easier.

As you contemplate this transition, remember you're not alone. Seeking support from family, friends, or professionals can ease the challenges and pave the way for a smoother move. Embrace the opportunity to redefine how you wish to live your life, setting goals that align with your current needs and aspirations. Downsizing need not be seen solely as an end but rather as a fresh beginning, bringing with it unexpected pleasures and the chance to appreciate life in a more intentional, present-minded way. With thoughtful planning and openness to change, this move could very well lead to a more fulfilling chapter in your life.

Chapter 2

Planning Your Downsizing Journey

Planning your downsizing journey is all about preparing for a new phase in life that can bring both opportunities and challenges. Downsizing isn't just about reducing space; it's about rethinking how you live, what you need, and what you value the most. The decision to downsize often comes with mixed emotions, but it offers the chance to simplify daily life and focus on what truly matters. Whatever motivates that decision, downsizing requires thoughtful planning.

In this chapter, you'll explore how to effectively assess your current lifestyle needs and identify what fits in your next home without compromising comfort, setting the stage for a successful downsizing experience that enhances rather than disrupts your life.

Assessing Your Needs

Once you have decided on a new place to live, you must work out what your needs are when it comes to living space. Guidelines are beneficial when downsizing, helping streamline the decision-making process. Start with a comprehensive assessment of your current needs. Consider making a list of "must-have" features versus "nice-to-haves" to help prioritize. For instance, do you need a dedicated office space, or can a multipurpose area suffice? This kind of clarity aids in deciding which comforts you can't live without and where there might be room for compromise. Below, we look at some factors to consider when assessing your housing needs.

How Much Space Do You Really Need?

While downsizing, determining how much space you actually need is a critical step. It's important to start by understanding your current lifestyle requirements to identify what space and amenities are genuinely essential. Perhaps you're used to hosting family gatherings regularly; you might find that maintaining a dining area that accommodates guests remains a priority. On the other hand, if you rarely use your formal living room, it could be a space you're willing to let go of in your next home. Reflecting on how you use each part of your home—whether it's a hobby room, a spacious kitchen, or an expansive backyard—will guide your decisions.

Think Long Term

Considering long-term implications ensures your new home will serve you well into the future. This includes contemplating your needs as you age and any accessibility features you may require later on. For example, single-story homes or those with minimal stairs can prevent potential mobility challenges down the road. Even if mobility isn't currently a concern, planning and anticipating such issues can save future upheaval. It's also worth considering the proximity of your next home to healthcare facilities or public transport, especially if you anticipate having to give up driving at some point in the future.

Consider Your Daily Routine

Daily routines and their impact on your new lifestyle are another aspect to consider. Moving to a new neighborhood can significantly alter your routine, from changes in commuting distances to the overall vibe of the community. If you have a regular commute, ensuring your new location doesn't add stress to your daily life is crucial. Likewise, a neighborhood's atmosphere plays a significant role: An area bustling with activity might suit someone who enjoys social engagement, whereas a quieter suburb might appeal to those seeking peace. When visiting potential areas, take note of local amenities like grocery stores, parks, and recreational facilities, which can greatly influence your quality of life.

Take Your Budget Into Account

Financial constraints are often a key factor in housing decisions. Ensuring that your downsized home fits comfortably within your budget without stretching your resources too thin is essential. While a smaller home typically incurs lower maintenance costs, property taxes, and utility bills, it's still necessary to factor these expenses into your financial plan. It's not just about the initial purchase price; long-term affordability should also be considered, especially if your income will change, perhaps due to retirement. Additionally, consider the potential resale value of the property. Downsizing doesn't always mean planning to stay indefinitely—having a home with good market value keeps options open, whether for selling in the future or leaving an inheritance for loved ones.

Setting Realistic Goals and Timelines

It is important to set clear goals regarding what you want from the downsizing process. Establish flexible timelines (see Chapter 1 for an example) that allow adjustments for unexpected challenges. Here are some realistic goals to set when moving house:

- **Declutter:** Aim to sort through and minimize your belongings well in advance of the move.

- **Create a Packing Schedule**: Set specific deadlines for packing different rooms to keep yourself on track.

- **Budgeting**: Establish a budget for moving expenses, including packing supplies, moving services, and any deposits.

- **Notify Important Contacts**: Make a goal to inform utilities, banks, employers, and other important contacts about your new address by a certain date.

- **Complete Repairs and Cleaning**: If you're renting, set a timeline for any necessary repairs and cleaning tasks before leaving.

- **Understand the New Neighborhood**: Research the new area, including schools, public transport, and amenities, to feel more at home quickly.

- **Settle In**: Plan a timeline for unpacking and setting up your new space within a few days of the move.

- **Work Out if You Need to Do Any Repairs**: Evaluate whether your new home needs repairs, painting, or renovations and if they need to be done before or can be completed after you move in. You will need to account for these repairs in your moving timeline.

- **Connect With Neighbors**: Make it a goal to introduce yourself to neighbors shortly after moving in to foster a sense of community.

These goals will help ensure a smoother transition to your new home. Once the move is complete, the goal is to create a space that enhances your lifestyle while remaining practical and economically viable. By focusing on essentials, anticipating future needs, and carefully balancing emotional ties with practical decisions, you lay the groundwork for a successful transition. The journey of finding the right-size home isn't merely about reducing square footage; it's about enhancing your living experience and ensuring comfort and satisfaction now and in years to come.

Create a Step-by-Step Plan

Developing an actionable downsizing strategy requires a structured approach that helps alleviate the emotional and logistical challenges that often accompany this transition. Breaking down the process into distinct stages can make it feel less overwhelming, providing clear direction and a sense of accomplishment along the way. By making plans, you can track your progress and maintain momentum.

Develop Organizational Systems

Developing organizational systems is another crucial element of the downsizing strategy. When sorting belongings, categorize them based on necessity, emotional value, and practicality.

- **Necessity** refers to items required for your daily life or plans; classify these clearly and store them where easily accessible.

- **Emotional values** are connected to cherished belongings that hold significant sentimental meaning. You might want to preserve a limited number of these items to prevent clutter in your new home.

- **Practicality** is assessed by considering how often you use an item or if it holds any functional benefit in your downsized lifestyle. This systematization aids in maintaining clarity and focus while ensuring nothing is overlooked or underestimated.

Here are some effective organizational systems for downsizing. Implementing these organizational systems can streamline your downsizing efforts, making the process more manageable and efficient:

- **The Marie Kondo Method:**
    - **Spark Joy**: Evaluate each item based on whether it "sparks joy." Keep only items that bring happiness and serve a purpose.

- **Category-Based Decluttering**: Tackle decluttering by category (clothing, books, papers, etc.) rather than by room to ensure a comprehensive approach.

- **The 3-Box System**:
  - **Keep, Donate, Trash**: Use three boxes to sort items as you declutter. Label them accordingly and make decisions about each item as you go.

- **One-Year Rule**:
  - **Items You Haven't Used**: For each item, assess if you've used it in the past year. If not, consider donating or discarding it.

- **Digital Inventory**:
  - **Photographic Cataloging**: Take photos of items you want to sell or donate and create a digital inventory to track what you have, what you're parting with, and where each item will go.

- **Room-by-Room Plan**:
  - **Focus on One Room at a Time**: Create a checklist for each room, including categories like furniture, decor, clothing, and appliances, to systematically downsize and organize.

- **30-Day Declutter Challenge**:
  - **Daily Decluttering Goals**: In this challenge, remove one item on day one, two on day two, and continue increasing the number of items daily for 30 days.

- **The 80/20 Rule**:
  - **Focus on Usage**: Identify the 20% of your belongings that you use 80% of the time. Consider letting go of the remaining 80% that you rarely use.

- **Storage Solutions**:
  - **Multifunctional Furniture**: Invest in storage solutions like ottomans, coffee tables, and beds with built-in storage to maximize space and keep essential items organized.

- **Digital Decluttering**:
  - **File and Unsubscribe**: Organize digital files by creating folders and categories on your computer, and unsubscribe from unnecessary emails and digital subscriptions.
- **Timeline for Downsizing**:
  - **Set a Schedule**: Develop a timeline with specific deadlines for each stage of the downsizing process, helping to maintain motivation and focus.

Divide the Project Into Phases

Start by dividing the project into phases, such as decluttering, deciding what to keep or donate, selling or giving away unwanted items, and finally, moving and setting up your new space. Each phase should have its timeline, allowing for adequate time to complete each task without feeling rushed. For example, begin with rooms that are used less frequently, like basements or attics, before tackling everyday spaces like kitchens and living rooms. An example of the kinds of phases you might divide moving into is presented below:

1. **Planning Phase**:
   - Set a moving date.
   - Create a moving budget.
   - Research moving options (DIY, professional movers).

2. **Decluttering Phase**:
   - Go through belongings and decide what to keep, donate, sell, or discard.
   - Set a plan for each room—it is easy to forget smaller rooms, but these still take time. Examples include the laundry, basement, and garage.
   - Organize a garage sale if desired.

3. **Packing Phase**:
   - Gather packing supplies (boxes, tape, bubble wrap).
   - Start packing nonessential items first.

- Label boxes by room and contents.
- Make a list that has the number of the box and details of its contents so that in the future you know which box contains what items.

4. **Final Preparations Phase**:
   - Confirm moving details with professionals or helpers.
   - Notify utilities, mail services, and important contacts of your change of address.
   - Create an inventory of packed items.
   - Organize cleaning for your old house if you are not doing it yourself after the move.

5. **Moving Day Phase**:
   - Execute the move (load truck, transport items, unload).
   - Conduct a final walk-through of the old house.
   - Start unpacking essential items at the new location.

6. **Settling In Phase**:
   - Unpack and arrange your new space.
   - Set up utilities and services.
   - Explore the new neighborhood and introduce yourself to neighbors.

Each phase helps in organizing the process and making the move less stressful. Remember, these milestones are not set in stone, but they serve to keep you on track and motivated.

If you need further guidance as to how to plan your move, see Chapter 7 for our example checklist!

Give Everyone a Role

An essential aspect of a successful downsizing journey is involving family members or hiring professionals to help streamline tasks and facilitate decision-making. Assign specific roles based on skills, availability, and willingness to assist. Family members can be invaluable in sorting through sentimental items, sharing memories, and making collective decisions about heirlooms or family treasures. In cases where emotional attachments complicate decision-making, consider bringing in a neutral professional organizer or consultant to offer objective perspectives and guidance.

Here are examples of roles and responsibilities associated with moving house that can be assigned to any friends and family who want to help:

1. **Primary Coordinator:**
   - Organizes the entire moving process.
   - Creates timelines and checklists.
   - Communicates with all involved parties.

2. **Decluttering Manager:**
   - Oversees the sorting and decluttering of belongings.
   - Decides what to keep, donate, sell, or discard.
   - Arranges for donations or disposal of unwanted items.

3. **Packing Team Leader:**
   - Supervises the packing of items.
   - Ensures that boxes are labeled correctly.
   - Manages packing supplies and equipment.

4. **Logistics Planner:**
   - Arranges for transportation (renting a moving truck, hiring movers).
   - Coordinates the schedule for moving day.
   - Keeps track of essential items needed on moving day.

5. **Financial Coordinator:**
   - Manages the moving budget.
   - Tracks expenses and invoices.
   - Arranges payments for services secured.

6. **Utility Manager:**

- Notifies utility companies of the move.
- Ensures services are set up at the new home.
- Arranges for internet, cable, and other services.

7. **New Home Explorer**:
   - Researches the new neighborhood.
   - Identifies nearby amenities, schools, and public transportation.
   - Connects with new neighbors.

8. **Unpacking Supervisor**:
   - Leads the unpacking process after the move.
   - Organizes items in the new home.
   - Ensures essential items are accessible first.

Having clear roles and responsibilities can help streamline the moving process and reduce stress. Multiple roles can be performed by the same person if required.

Be Flexible

Flexibility is the cornerstone of any effective moving plan, particularly when transitioning to a smaller living space. Allow yourself more time than you think you need. Unexpected challenges, such as delays in selling your current home or finding suitable storage solutions, may arise. Being adaptable allows you to adjust your timelines and strategies as needed, mitigating potential stress. Embrace change as an opportunity for growth and actively encourage involvement from everyone participating, whether they're family members or hired professionals. This adaptability is crucial in today's fast-paced environment and ensures a smoother transition into the new chapter of your life (What are the three pillars of strategic planning: Building a solid foundation for success, 2024).

Involving Family

Navigating family involvement during a downsizing transition can be a challenging yet rewarding process. Below, we look at ways of involving family with your move and managing any divergent perspectives that might emerge at this time.

Practice Open Communication

When planning to downsize, it's crucial to communicate openly with family members about your intentions and seek their thoughts on the matter. This approach addresses concerns and aligns expectations, fostering a more harmonious transition. For instance, discussing the reasons behind the decision to downsize can help family members understand the motivations driving this change.

Engaging in open communication also provides an opportunity to gather valuable feedback. Family members might have insights or suggestions that hadn't been considered, providing a fresh perspective on how to navigate the downsizing process effectively. It is important to create an environment where everyone feels comfortable expressing their viewpoints. This openness paves the way for collective problem-solving, making it easier to address any apprehensions or obstacles that may arise.

Balance Emotional Attachments With Practical Decisions

Balancing emotional attachments and practical decisions is another critical aspect of downsizing. Personal belongings often carry sentimental value, making it difficult to part with them. Prioritizing what to keep based on necessity and practicality over emotional attachment can ease the decision-making process. One approach involves setting aside a special day to go through items together as a family and sharing stories and memories before deciding what to keep, discard, sell, or donate. This practice not only honors the sentimental value of possessions but also motivates practical decision-making.

In cases where differing opinions or disagreements arise, having conflict resolution strategies in place is paramount. Disagreements may arise when family members have varying ideas about which items should be kept or how the process should be handled. Establishing clear strategies for managing these conflicts can prevent tensions from escalating. One effective strategy is to designate a neutral mediator within the family who can facilitate discussions and ensure that all voices are heard.

Dealing with family members who have been using your home as free storage can be a sensitive issue during downsizing. Here are strategies to approach this situation:

1. **Open Communication**: Initiate a conversation with family members about your plans to downsize. Be honest about your need for space and your desire to reclaim your home.

2. **Set Boundaries**: Clearly explain your new boundaries regarding storage in your home. Let them know that you will no longer be able to accommodate their belongings.

3. **Create a Timeline**: Give a reasonable timeline for them to retrieve their items. This allows them to prepare and reduces the chance of lingering belongings.

4. **Organize a Sorting Session**: Invite family members to help sort through their items. This can be a collaborative effort where they decide what to keep, throw away, or donate.

5. **Offer to Help**: Extend your assistance in helping them find suitable storage solutions outside your home, such as renting a storage unit or using their own space.

6. **Decide What to Keep**: If they agree to donate or discard items, offer to help identify valuable donations or trash for convenient disposal.

7. **Set Up a "Return Day"**: Plan a specific day for returning their items. This creates a sense of urgency and encourages them to act on their possessions.

8. **Suggest Charitable Donations**: If they are unable to take back their items, suggest donating them to charities, explaining that it helps those in need.

9. **Document the Process**: Keep a record of what items are being returned or donated for transparency. This helps avoid misunderstandings and provides clarity for both parties.

10. **Be Firm but Compassionate**: While it's important to be empathetic and understanding, be firm in your decision. Emphasize that reclaiming your space is essential for your well-being.

By approaching the situation with empathy and clear communication, you can successfully navigate the process of dealing with family members' belongings while downsizing your home.

Highlighting the benefits that come with downsizing can also help gain support from reluctant family members. Emphasizing potential benefits such as financial savings from lower living costs, the reutilization of unwanted items through donation or sale, and a positive lifestyle change can illustrate the advantages of the downsizing process for everyone involved. These benefits often extend beyond the immediate family, creating opportunities for community engagement through charitable donations and environmentally friendly practices by reducing consumerism and waste.

Furthermore, reassuring family members that downsizing does not mean erasing the past but rather cherishing and preserving important memories can alleviate concerns. Consider creating a digital photo archive or scrapbook documenting cherished items before they are sold or donated. This allows the family to retain the memory of the possessions without being burdened by their physical presence, offering a compromise that respects both emotional connections and practical needs.

What If They Don't Want My Excess Items?

It may seem that giving away old items to friends and family is the ideal solution. However, sometimes they may not want your excess items. Handling the situation when family or friends do not want items you're giving away during downsizing can be challenging. Here are some strategies to manage this scenario:

1. **Be Understanding**: Acknowledge that not everyone may want your items, and that's okay. Everyone has different preferences and needs.

2. **Explain Your Intentions**: Share your reasons for downsizing and why you need to find new homes for your belongings. This can help them understand your perspective.

3. **Host a Giveaway Event**: Consider organizing a small gathering where you showcase the items you're giving away. Friends and family may find something they want when they see it in person.

4. **Set a Deadline**: If certain items need to be cleared out, establish a timeline for when you plan to donate or dispose of them. Communicate this deadline to family and friends.

5. **Stay Firm but Flexible**: While it's important to be open to suggestions, maintain your boundaries. If they are not interested in taking items, be ready to move forward with your plans.

6. **Involve a Third Party**: If appropriate, ask a neutral friend or family member to help mediate the situation. Their perspective can lighten the conversation and encourage acceptance.

7. **Accept Help With the Process**: Invite friends or family to assist in the decluttering process. Sometimes, their help can bring new perspectives on items that they may find valuable.

8. **Let Go of Guilt**: Remind yourself that it's okay for your belongings to find new homes elsewhere. Focus on the benefits of downsizing and creating a more organized space.

By approaching the situation with empathy and a focus on finding solutions, you can navigate the challenges of giving away items without added stress or conflict.

Summary

As you think about downsizing, it's important to remember that this process isn't just about getting rid of things; it's about crafting a new way of living that's both simple and fulfilling. Here, we've explored how to plan and organize your move to make your transition smooth and less stressful. By considering what truly matters in your home and recognizing future needs, you lay the foundation for purchasing and creating a space that supports your lifestyle goals. It's essential to look at the bigger picture, not just focusing on immediate changes but also anticipating how your choices will affect you down the road. We are here to guide you with empathy and clarity, ensuring your downsizing journey is rewarding.

Remember, involving family and friends in planning the downsizing process can bring fresh perspectives and emotional support. Downsizing is as much about embracing change as it is about letting go. Having open discussions about what you hope to achieve during the planning process and acknowledging the feelings attached to certain possessions can help everyone involved move forward together. Flexibility is key—being able to adapt your plans when unexpected challenges pop up will make the process feel more manageable. In the end, it's all about finding joy in simplifying your life, creating a home that feels right for you, and stepping confidently into this new chapter with excitement and peace of mind.

Chapter 3

Decluttering 101 – Letting Go With Compassion

Letting go of clutter is about making space for what truly matters. We often accumulate a collection of items that not only fill our homes but also our minds. These belongings can represent memories, aspirations, and sometimes even status. However, when they become clutter, they can overshadow the tranquility and simplicity we crave as we transition to new stages of life, like retirement or an empty nest. The process of decluttering encourages us to take a compassionate look at these possessions and decide which ones still serve our present needs. It's a journey that merges practicality with emotions, allowing us to set the wheels of change in motion. By understanding the core principles of decluttering, we set the stage for creating a home environment that aligns more closely with who we are today, rather than clinging to the past.

In this chapter, we look at the essential strategies that make decluttering both manageable and meaningful. Here, we encourage you to let go and embrace a lifestyle that prioritizes present joy and utility over accumulation, helping you move toward creating a living space that's organized, functional, and reflective of your current life.

Principles and Methods of Decluttering and Decision-Making

Sorting, discarding, donating, and selling are key principles in the journey to a clutter-free home. As you begin your decluttering adventure, understanding these concepts will help simplify the decision-making process and ensure that your living space becomes more organized and meaningful.

Sorting

The process of decluttering begins with sorting, which is all about categorizing items based on their function, necessity, and frequency of use. Imagine stepping into your garage or a crowded kitchen cabinet and feeling overwhelmed by the sheer volume of stuff. The first step is to sort through these items, grouping them into categories such as "tools," "cutlery," or "appliances." This helps in visualizing the extent of each category and makes it easier to decide what really deserves a spot in your home. By identifying duplicate items, such as two immersion blenders, you can also start to see where simplification is possible. Remember, the goal is not just to tidy up but to make informed choices about what best serves your current lifestyle.

Discarding

Discarding involves the thoughtful evaluation of each item in your home. Each belonging should be considered for its current and potential future usefulness. Ask yourself: Is this something I use daily? Does it serve a purpose, or has it become just another piece in my collection of unused objects? Discarding isn't just about getting rid of things; it's a process that enables you to learn from your past purchases and decisions. Holding onto an unworn jacket because it was expensive doesn't help if it's just taking up space. Letting go is a skill, one that grows stronger each time you practice it. As Marie Kondo notes in her KonMari Method™, finish discarding before storing items permanently to get an accurate sense of your true needs (*What is the KonMari method?*, 2024).

Donating

Donating offers a rewarding opportunity to give a second life to items. Just because something no longer fits into your life doesn't mean it won't fit into someone else's. Take those books that you've already read or those clothes that don't quite match your style anymore. Donating these items can be incredibly fulfilling, knowing they will find new homes where they are appreciated and used. Moreover, donating helps reduce environmental waste, as items are repurposed rather than piling up in landfills. So, next time you're cleaning out your closet, think about how your past possessions might become someone else's treasure.

Keep or Donate?

How do I decide whether to keep or donate an item? Often, we struggle to decide what is worth keeping and what should be donated or recycled. To decide whether to keep or discard items in your home, you can follow these steps:

- **Assess Need**: Consider if you actually use the item regularly. If you haven't used it in the past year, it might be time to let it go.

- **Evaluate Condition**: Check the item's condition. Is it broken, damaged, or worn out? If it's not in good shape and cannot be repaired, consider discarding it.

- **Sentimental Value**: Think about the emotional attachment you have to the item. If it holds significant sentimental value and brings you joy, you may want to keep it.

- **Space Consideration:** Reflect on whether you have enough space for the item. If your space is limited, it might be necessary to let go of things that are less important.

- **Functionality**: Determine if the item serves a purpose. If it no longer fits your lifestyle or serves a function, it may be time to discard it.

- **Number of Similar Items**: Consider if you have multiple items serving the same purpose. If you have too many similar items, keep only the best or most meaningful ones.

- **Future Use**: Ask yourself if you might need it in the future. If you don't foresee using it again, you may want to let it go.

- **Donation, Selling, or Recycling**: For items in good condition that you don't want anymore, consider donating, selling, or recycling instead of throwing them away.

By going through these steps systematically, you can make more informed decisions about what to keep and what to discard.

Starting Small and Managing Sentimental Values

Embarking on the journey of decluttering your living space can be a daunting but rewarding process. It's about creating an environment that reflects your current lifestyle and brings a sense of peace and order into your daily life. However, the emotional aspect of decluttering, particularly dealing with sentimental items, requires a gentle approach focused on compassion and clarity.

Starting small is key to preventing the process from becoming overwhelming. Choose one room or category at a time. This could be a kitchen, bedroom, or even a specific category of items like clothing or books. Focusing on just one area helps you see progress more quickly, which in turn motivates you to continue. For many, beginning with commonly used areas such as kitchens or bedrooms provides immediate benefits. A tidy kitchen makes meal preparation smoother and less stressful, while a decluttered bedroom promotes restful sleep—both essential aspects of daily life.

Here are some steps to declutter one room of your house effectively. You can practice these when moving house and to maintain your new home once your move is complete:

1. **Set a Clear Goal**: Determine what you want to achieve in this room. Do you want more space, better organization, or simply a tidier appearance?

2. **Gather Supplies**: Get boxes or bags for items you want to keep, donate, recycle, or discard.

3. **Empty the Room**: If possible, remove everything from the room to get a clear view of the space.

4. **Categorize Items**: As you take items out, sort them into categories such as clothing, books, paperwork, or decor.

5. **Evaluate Each Item**: Go through each item and ask yourself:

   - Do I use it?

   - Do I love it?

   - Is it in good condition?

6. **Make Decisions**: For each item, decide to keep, donate, recycle, or throw away. Be honest about what you really need.

7. **Organize Kept Items**: Arrange the items you're keeping in an organized manner. Use bins, shelves, or drawers to keep everything tidy.

8. **Establish a System**: Create a system for maintaining the decluttered space. This could involve regular clean-up schedules or designating specific spots for each item.

9. **Dispose of Unwanted Items**: Take the donation or recycling bags to their respective locations as soon as possible to avoid second-guessing your decisions.

10. **Enjoy the Space**: Take a moment to appreciate your decluttered room and enjoy the newfound space and order.

By following these steps, you can effectively declutter and transform one room in your house, either to streamline your life or in preparation for moving house.

Once you've selected your starting point, whether that be a room or a set of items, proceed with a mixture of practicality and empathy, especially when tackling sentimental items. Sentimental possessions often carry memories and emotional significance, making it challenging to let them go. As you sort through these objects, ask yourself why each item holds meaning for you. Consider ways to honor its memory without having to keep the physical object. Perhaps a photo of the item or writing down the memory associated with it can suffice, allowing you to preserve the sentiment while freeing up physical space.

It's okay to remember all the feelings associated with a particular item—whether it makes you feel happy or sad. Don't be afraid to go back in time, relive the moment—be happy or shed a tear. Then think of how you can recreate the memory you are trying to keep without the physical item. If it is too hard, then maybe keeping the item in a special memory box or space is the best thing. These should only be for the most precious of memories.

You or your family members may also hold onto items because you believe them to be valuable. If this is the case, undertake a quick search on Google to get an estimate of value—often, your "valuable" item will turn out to be worth far less than you think.

Decision-Making Strategies

When you're navigating decluttering, it can often feel extremely challenging. But with the right strategies and a mindset that encourages gratitude, this process can become more fulfilling. Below, we look at decision-making strategies you can apply to effectively navigate the decluttering process.

Visualization

By visualizing a clutter-free environment, you boost your motivation to make decisive choices. Imagine walking into a space where everything has its place, where surfaces are clear, and you can breathe easily. Visualization exercises can be powerful in helping you connect with the peace and calm that comes from a tidy home. These visions serve as reminders of the goals you're working toward, making it easier to stay focused and determined during the decluttering process.

Here's a visualization exercise to help you create a tidy, organized home:

1. **Find a Quiet Space**: Choose a comfortable and quiet place where you can relax without distractions. Sit or lie down in a comfortable position.

2. **Close Your Eyes**: Gently close your eyes and take a few deep breaths. Inhale slowly through your nose, hold for a moment, and exhale through your mouth. Allow your body to relax with each breath.

3. **Visualize Your Home**: Imagine the entrance to your home. Visualize the front door and picture yourself stepping inside. As you enter, notice how you feel in this space.

4. **Picture Each Room**: Begin to visualize each room in your home, one at a time. Start with the living room. Envision it tidy and organized—sofa pillows neatly arranged, no clutter on the coffee table, and a clear pathway to move around.

5. **Incorporate Colors and Textures**: Imagine the colors of the walls, the textures of the furniture, and the overall ambiance of

the room. Picture yourself enjoying this serene and inviting space.

6. **Move to Other Rooms**: Continue this visualization for each room in your home. Picture the kitchen—clean countertops, organized cabinets, and a sense of calm as you move around. Visualize the bedroom—neatly made bed, clothes organized, and peaceful decor.

7. **Imagining Organization**: Envision how each item in your home has a designated place. Picture drawers that slide open to reveal neatly folded clothes, shelves that display books and decor in a harmonious way, and storage bins that keep items contained and out of sight.

8. **Sense of Accomplishment**: Allow yourself to feel the satisfaction and accomplishment of having a tidy home. Imagine how it feels to invite friends over to a clean, organized space. Embrace the positive emotions that come with this visualization.

9. **Create a Vision Board (optional)**: If you enjoy creative activities, consider creating a vision board based on your visualization. Cut out images or phrases from magazines that represent the organized spaces you've imagined and place them on a board as a reminder.

10. **Come Back to Reality**: When you're ready, slowly bring your awareness back to the present moment. Open your eyes and take a few deep breaths.

By practicing this visualization regularly, you can reinforce the desire to create a tidy, organized home and feel motivated to take actionable steps toward achieving that vision.

The "One-Year Rule"

The "one-year rule" offers a practical guideline when determining whether a possession is still necessary in your life. If an item hasn't been used in a year, it's worth questioning its value to you now.

Here's how it works:

1. **Time Frame:** The rule operates on a one-year time frame, which provides a clear benchmark for evaluating items in your home.

2. **Evaluation Criteria:** When assessing each item, ask yourself:
   - Have I used this item in the last year?
   - Is there a specific reason I haven't used it?
   - Do I foresee needing it soon?

3. **Types of Items:** The one-year rule can apply to various categories of items, including clothing, kitchen gadgets, tools, books, and decor.

4. **Exceptions:** While the rule is generally effective, there may be exceptions. Items used seasonally (like holiday decorations) or those with significant sentimental value may not need to be discarded, even if they haven't been used in the past year.

5. **Clarity and Focus:** By applying the one-year rule, you can reduce decision fatigue and create a more streamlined approach to decluttering. It encourages you to be more mindful about what you keep and why.

6. **Promotes a Minimalist Mindset:** This rule fosters a minimalist approach, helping you focus on keeping only those items that serve a purpose or bring you joy.

7. **Actionable Steps:** When decluttering, create a plan to go through your belongings by category or room, apply the one-year rule to each item, and make decisions on what to keep, donate, sell, or discard.

Incorporating the one-year rule into your decluttering efforts can help simplify the process and create a more organized living space.

This method encourages objectivity, helping you decide if you genuinely need something or are holding onto it out of habit. Decluttering through this lens not only makes practical sense but empowers you to make confident choices aligned with your current needs and aspirations

The "One-In, One-Out Rule" can help maintain balance in your newfound clarity (*From chaos to calm: Effective decluttering strategies,* 2024). Every time something new enters your home, something old should make its way out. This simple guideline prevents the accumulation of unnecessary items and encourages mindful purchasing habits, so your environment stays spacious and uncluttered.

The "Joy Test"

The "joy test" method was made famous by Marie Kondo. This approach emphasizes keeping only those items that evoke happiness or have a practical role in your everyday life. When you hold an object, notice how it makes you feel. Does it spark joy? Does it bring back positive memories or emotions, or does it leave you indifferent? This is not just about emotional attachment; it's about ensuring that every item you own adds value to your life, whether through utility or sentiment. The practicality test is just as critical. Ask if an item is useful: Do you need it? If your answer is a resounding no, perhaps it's time to let it go.

This approach to decluttering encourages a mindful relationship with your belongings, fostering gratitude and respect for what you choose to keep. As you sort, discard, donate, and apply the joy test, remember this process is about creating a space that reflects who you truly are at this stage of life. By letting go of items that no longer serve you, both physically and emotionally, you open room for growth, allowing your environment to support your ideal lifestyle.

The Importance of Gratitude

Incorporating gratitude into your decluttering routine can significantly shift how you view your belongings. Instead of seeing items solely as physical objects, try focusing on the memories they evoke. For instance, if you come across an old T-shirt from a family reunion, rather than getting caught up in whether you should keep it just because it's familiar, reflect on the joyful time shared with loved ones. This practice allows you to honor the memory without feeling compelled to hold onto every tangible reminder. It's about appreciating the moments these items represent rather than the items themselves.

Shifting your perspective from material possessions to cherished experiences and relationships can enhance your emotional well-being. When decluttering, ask yourself how much value each item adds to your life beyond its physical presence. Does it remind you of a special bond or a meaningful adventure? If not, let it go knowing that the true treasures lie in those who share your life and the experiences you gather together.

For many, it might be beneficial to keep a gratitude journal documenting the process. Write down thoughts for the items you decide to part with, acknowledging the role they played in your life up until now. This act of gratitude can bring closure, making it easier to release them. Gratitude journaling also reinforces positive feelings around decluttering, transforming what could be a daunting task into a reflective and enjoyable experience.

Summary

As we wrap up this exploration of decluttering, it's clear that it involves more than just sorting and discarding items. It's about understanding the emotional ties we have to our belongings and learning to let go in a way that makes space for what truly matters. Whether you're tackling sentimental keepsakes, everyday clutter, or preparing to downsize, approaching this process with empathy and compassion is essential. Remember, you're not just creating physical space but also paving the way for greater mental clarity and peace in your living environment.

Embarking on this path can feel overwhelming, especially when faced with decisions about items tied to cherished memories. But know that each step you take, no matter how small, contributes to crafting a home that supports your current lifestyle and aspirations. Embrace the joy of giving objects new life through donation and appreciate the simplicity of an uncluttered space. By focusing on gratitude and smart decision-making strategies, you'll find that decluttering becomes less of a chore and more of a transformative experience.

Chapter 4

Practical Tools and Techniques for Decluttering

Decluttering your living space is a transformative process that can truly change how you experience your home. It's not just about creating more room; it's about crafting an environment that supports your lifestyle, especially as life transitions like retirement or downsizing come into play. The act of decluttering involves saying goodbye to items that no longer serve a purpose and welcoming a sense of order and simplicity. It's a step toward making your surroundings reflect who you are now and who you want to be in the future. Every item you keep should earn its place by adding genuine value to your life. This approach allows your home to evolve with your needs, becoming a comforting sanctuary rather than a storeroom for memories.

Here, we dive into practical tools and techniques that make the decluttering journey easier and more effective. By engaging with these ideas, you'll learn how to maintain balance in your home, adapting seamlessly to life's changes while holding onto what truly matters.

Creating a Sorting System

Creating a clutter-free environment becomes far more manageable when you have a structured sorting method. This section will guide you through developing such a method, focusing on color-coding, labeling, and systematic organization. These strategies can transform the task of decluttering into a more engaging and rewarding experience.

Color-Coding

Color-coding is an effective technique to visually categorize items. By assigning specific colors to different categories or priorities, decision-making becomes much easier. Consider using colored labels to distinguish between items you wish to keep, donate, or discard. This visual system not only simplifies your sorting process but also helps prevent the feeling of being overwhelmed by having to make too many decisions at once. For instance, items marked with green could represent essentials that are ready to be kept, while blue might signify things you plan to donate, thus streamlining the transition (*Spring organizing using color coding labels*, 2024).

Within your wardrobe, implementing color codes can make selecting an outfit an enjoyable activity. Assign colors like light blue for summer clothes and dark green for winter wear. This method not only adds a splash of color to your closet but also speeds up the morning routine. No longer will you have to sift through piles to find that perfect dress for a sunny day. It's right there in the designated section, making your mornings just a tad less hectic.

Downsizing can feel daunting without a proper plan. Fortunately, a color-coded system eases this transition by clearly marking what needs to be kept, discarded, donated, or sold. Imagine going through your attic, surrounded by boxes filled with memories. With a color-coded system, those memories come to life in a new home or shine brighter with you in a smaller space. This method doesn't just help in physically organizing your items but emotionally supports you in letting go of what's no longer necessary (*Spring organizing using color coding labels*, 2024).

Labeling

Labeling plays a crucial role in clarifying item details, ownership, and locations. When used properly, labels help you achieve a well-managed environment. Start with clear, concise descriptions; ensure that they're easy to read and durable. Using fine-tip permanent markers guarantees labels remain legible over time. Strategically place these labels where they are easily visible and accessible. For example, position them at the front of storage containers or the upper corners of documents to quickly identify the contents at a glance.

For maximum efficiency, always clean the surface before applying a label. This simple step ensures better adhesion and longevity. Consistency in placement also reduces confusion later on. Picture opening a kitchen cabinet and immediately spotting a labeled jar of spices. Not only does this save time, but it also enhances your cooking experience, allowing you to focus on creativity rather than chaos.

The artistry in labeling goes beyond words. Incorporating symbols or icons can further simplify identification, especially if you're dealing with a diverse range of items. A heart symbol next to gifts or an arrow indicating frequently used tools can provide quick cues. The goal is to create a system so intuitive that it feels second nature, making everyday tasks almost effortless.

Essential Decluttering Tools

Equipping yourself with the right tools is crucial for streamlining the decluttering process. Entering this journey can be overwhelming, but breaking down tasks and using specific items can greatly ease the workload. As you venture into decluttering, remember that your goal is not just to remove excess items but to create a sustainable lifestyle change. By using the foundational tools of boxes, bags, storage bins, and apps, you equip yourself to tackle decluttering both physically and digitally. These tools do more than organize your space; they streamline the entire process, helping you maintain a harmonious home environment with ease and confidence. Here's how to make it manageable.

Bags and Storage Boxes

Always incorporate bags into your decluttering arsenal. Sturdy bags are vital for segregating items that are destined for donation, recycling, or disposal. The flexibility of bags makes them ideal for carrying lighter, non-fragile items such as clothing or paper. They also keep these items out of sight, which lessens emotional attachment and helps in making quicker decisions about letting go. Opaque bags are particularly effective because once something goes into them, it becomes less visible and easier to part with.

Create a clear plan for sorting through your belongings by utilizing boxes. These handy containers are not just for storage; they serve as temporary holding areas while you decide what to keep, donate, sell, or discard. This method allows for an organized approach and minimizes the chaos usually associated with decluttering. For example, have separate boxes labeled "Keep," "Donate," "Sell," and "Discard." This will help quickly identify where items should go, reducing indecision and helping you move through items systematically.

Investing in quality storage bins is another essential step for achieving long-term organization. Unlike temporary solutions, good storage bins offer protection and accessibility, allowing you to safeguard valuable items you've chosen to keep. Clear bins are especially useful as they provide visibility, so you can see what's inside without opening them, saving time when you need to retrieve something. Consider bins with stackable lids to maximize space efficiency. Think of these bins as a permanent tool in maintaining order, ensuring that your living environment remains clutter-free.

Leverage Technology

In today's digital age, technology can also significantly aid the decluttering process. Digital apps can track your progress, manage inventory, and even assist in planning tasks. If you visit your favorite app store, you will find apps like inventory managers that offer features such as item categorization, reminder notifications, and data syncing across devices, ensuring you never lose track of what has been sorted. Many apps allow you to create lists or set goals, providing a structured timeline to achieve a decluttered home. These digital tools not only enhance efficiency but also help monitor ongoing efforts to prevent future buildup of clutter, which is key to maintaining a tidy space over the long term (*The joy of paperless post and party planning*, 2019).

Moreover, being digitally organized complements physical organization efforts. Just as you would organize a room, managing your digital files can bring clarity and peace of mind. Uninstall any unused apps to free up space on your devices, just like removing unnecessary items from your home. Use calendar systems that sync across all your gadgets to ensure you stay on top of scheduled decluttering sessions. This turns a daunting task into a manageable routine.

Decluttering Strategies for Specific Areas of the Home

Here are various decluttering strategies tailored to different parts of the home:

Living Room

- **The Four-Box Method**: Label four boxes as "Keep," "Donate," "Sell," and "Trash." Sort items into these boxes to streamline the decision-making process.

- **Surface Clear-Out**: Start by clearing surfaces like tables and shelves. Keep only essential items and decorative pieces that bring you joy.

- **One In, One Out Rule**: For every new item brought in, remove an old one to maintain balance and prevent clutter from accumulating.

Kitchen

- **Pantry Purge**: Empty your pantry and check expiration dates. Dispose of expired items and categorize remaining food by type for easy access.

- **Drawer Dividers**: Use drawer dividers to organize utensils and kitchen gadgets, making it easier to see and access what you need.

- **Appliance Assessment**: Evaluate small appliances. Keep only those you use regularly, and consider donating or selling unused devices.

Bedroom

- **Seasonal Rotation**: Rotate clothing seasonally. Store out-of-season clothes in bins to free up space in your closet.

- **Nightstand Clean-Up**: Clear out your nightstand drawer and keep only essential items like a lamp, a book, and a sleep mask.

Bathroom

- **Medicine Cabinet Audit**: Check expiration dates on medications and toiletries. Safely dispose of expired items and donate unused products.

- **Travel-Sized Item Use-Up**: Use up travel-sized products before purchasing new full-sized items to reduce excess clutter.

- **Drawer and Shelf Organization**: Use baskets or dividers to keep similar items together and easily accessible.

Home Office

- **Paper Declutter**: Go through papers and categorize them into "Keep," "Shred," and "Recycle." Go digital whenever possible to reduce paper.

- **Digital Declutter**: Organize files on your computer by creating folders, deleting unnecessary documents, and backing up important files.

- **Set Time Limits**: Allocate specific time blocks to declutter your workspace, focusing on one area at a time for efficiency.

Garage or Storage Area

- **Categorize and Zone**: Sort items into categories (tools, seasonal decor, sports equipment) and dedicate specific zones for each category to keep things organized.

- **Vertical Storage Solutions**: Utilize wall space with shelves or pegboards for tools and equipment, freeing up floor space and improving accessibility.

- **Annual Clean-Out**: Plan an annual decluttering day to assess and organize storage areas, ensuring they remain functional and clutter-free.

Closets

- **The Hanger Method**: Turn all hangers in your closet backward. Once you wear an item, return its hanger to the standard position. After a certain period, donate items still hanging backward.

- **Categorize by Type**: Organize clothes by type (shirts, pants, dresses) or by color for visual appeal and ease of access.

- **Incorporate Clear Bins**: Use clear bins to store seasonal or rarely used items, making it easy to see what you have without digging around.

Using these decluttering strategies can help you tackle different areas of your home systematically, promoting a more organized and inviting living space.

Handling Paperwork and Digital Clutter

Managing your physical and digital documents doesn't have to be a daunting task. Once you get the hang of a few practical strategies, it can become an integral part of maintaining an organized and serene environment in your home or office. Let's dive into some effective methods for managing both paper and electronic files as part of the decluttering and downsizing process.

Use Scanning Technology

First up, consider using scanning technology. Scanning technology refers to methods and systems used to capture data or images from physical objects and convert them into a digital format. This process involves converting physical documents into digital files using flatbed scanners, handheld scanners, multifunction printers, or even by using your phone to take photos.

Think of all those piles of paper documents just gathering dust in your drawers and cabinets. By converting these into a digital format, you dramatically reduce the amount of physical clutter in your space. Scanning apps and devices allow you to create digital copies of newsletters, receipts, and even handwritten notes. These digital versions don't just save space; they also make it easier for you to find what you're looking for with just a quick search on your computer or smartphone.

Destroy Documents

Addressing document destruction is equally critical. When disposing of sensitive information or confidential papers, shredding is the way to go. It ensures that your private details aren't left vulnerable to identity theft or unauthorized access. Shredders come in various sizes and capabilities, from small personal models to heavy-duty office machines. If you prefer not to handle shredding yourself, many office supply stores offer secure shredding services that can handle larger volumes efficiently. Following standardized document destruction protocols is essential to ensure compliance and protect against data breaches. For example, old tax records and bank statements need to be shredded securely after their retention period. Tax records should be kept for at least three years, while bank statements should be kept for at least one year, or three years if they are related to tax-deductible expenses. This may vary depending on what county you are in, so always double-check! You'll have peace of mind knowing that your personal information is out of reach for anyone who might exploit it.

Also, establish regular review schedules. Just as we maintain our homes, our digital spaces demand upkeep too. Set aside a specific time each month to go through your files and emails, discarding what you no longer need. Regularly deleting unnecessary items prevents digital file overload and keeps your devices running smoothly. Apply a similar principle to your physical documents, ensuring that outdated paperwork finds its way to the shredder instead of staying in storage indefinitely. This routine check-in helps prevent clutter from reaccumulating and ensures you're always working with the most up-to-date information.

Organize Information

To properly declutter, you need to organize information, both physical and digital. Organizing important documents systematically involves more than just placing them in neat piles. Consider categorizing them by type and purpose. For instance, family medical records can be grouped separately from financial documents or personal letters. Physically, use folders or file boxes labeled clearly to keep things tidy and accessible.

Digitally, you'll want to create a structured folder system on your computer or in cloud storage. Naming conventions are key; think about descriptive titles and a logical hierarchy. For example, you could create a main folder titled "Household" with subfolders like "Bills," "Warranties," and "Insurance." This method makes retrieval swift and efficient while minimizing time spent searching through unrelated files.

Summary

In this chapter, we've provided effective techniques and essential tools to help you conquer clutter and transform your living space into a more manageable and stress-free environment. By embracing strategies like color-coding and labeling, you're not just organizing your surroundings but making decisions easier and decluttering feel less overwhelming. These methods bring clarity and joy to everyday tasks, from picking out clothes to managing a well-ordered kitchen.

As you equip yourself with the right tools, such as boxes for sorting or digital apps for tracking progress, you'll find that maintaining order becomes second nature. Dealing with both physical and digital clutter means adopting systems that adapt to your evolving needs, ensuring your home remains welcoming and efficient. Remember, the goal isn't about achieving the perfect space but creating a sustainable lifestyle change that supports your happiness and peace of mind. With each small step toward decluttering, you're not just freeing up space—you're opening up new possibilities for a more fulfilling life. Remember, the downsizing challenge does not just help you move house but helps you remain clutter-free in your new home!

Chapter 5

Selling, Donating, and Recycling – Where Does It All Go?

Sorting through our belongings and deciding where everything should go can be both a daunting and liberating experience. Whether we're looking to sell, donate, or recycle, each decision reflects how we manage our physical spaces and engage with our communities and the environment. Letting go of items doesn't just clear space in our homes; it offers a chance to help others, make some extra money, and contribute to a more sustainable world. As we journey through this process, we must tailor our actions to fit personal needs and values while ensuring that what we let go of doesn't simply end up as someone else's problem or unnecessary waste.

Below, we look at various approaches to responsibly selling, donating, and recycling items. This chapter will guide you through making thoughtful decisions in downsizing and aligning practical actions with a broader commitment to community welfare and environmental health.

Options for Selling Items

Selling unwanted items can be both a practical way to declutter your home and an opportunity to earn some extra cash. Given the diverse options available, choosing the right method for selling will largely depend on factors such as the number of items, types of goods, and your own availability and willingness to engage with the sales process. Garage sales and online marketplaces are well-suited for those preferring a DIY approach and who desire control over pricing and selling. Conversely, consignment shops and estate sales may appeal more to individuals seeking ease of process and professional handling of sales. As we explore various avenues for selling, it's important to choose the method that best aligns with your needs and circumstances—here are some effective strategies to consider.

Garage Sales

A garage sale is a sale of unwanted items, typically held in a person's garage or yard. It often includes various household goods, clothing, toys, and other items that the seller no longer needs. The goal is to declutter and make some extra money by selling these items to neighbors and passersby at low prices.

Garage sales offer the opportunity to sell multiple items at once. This approach is particularly beneficial for those looking to sell a large volume of items quickly, as it allows for direct interaction with potential buyers. The casual nature of garage sales makes them appealing for both sellers and buyers. To maximize success, plan your sale on a weekend to attract more visitors and price items reasonably to encourage bulk purchases.

In preparation for a garage sale, follow our simple guide!

- Start by gathering all items you wish to sell and organizing them into categories such as clothing, kitchenware, toys, or tools.

- Advertise your sale throughout your neighborhood using flyers and online community boards.

- Set up tables or categories of goods.

- Have cash available for change. It may also be worth organizing a card machine like Square, as many people use cards exclusively these days.

- Work out what will happen to the goods if they don't sell; this will help you remain rational about the price even if it seems low (something is better than nothing).

- Enlist friends and family members to help out. Keep safe: don't let strangers into your home.

- On the day of your sale, having clear pricing labels and a friendly demeanor can go a long way in attracting buyers.

Remember, flexibility in negotiations can lead to a successful and profitable day.

Online Marketplaces

For those aiming to reach a broader audience, online marketplaces like eBay and Craigslist or others popular in your region are excellent options. These platforms allow users to list items for a wider audience beyond their immediate locality, increasing the chances of finding interested buyers. While eBay's auction-style listings may attract higher bids, especially for unique or high-demand items, Craigslist offers opportunities for fixed-price listings with local interactions.

When venturing into online selling, consider taking clear, high-quality images of each item, accompanied by detailed descriptions to give potential buyers confidence in their purchases. Ensure you're aware of any shipping requirements and costs if applicable, as these factors play a significant role in determining your item's final selling price and profitability. Be mindful of safety when arranging in-person transactions through sites like Craigslist, opting for public places to meet buyers whenever possible.

Consignment Shops

Consignment shops represent another viable avenue for selling unwanted items without directly handling the sales process yourself. These shops typically specialize in specific categories, such as clothing, furniture, or vintage goods, and take care of marketing and pricing your items, which can save time and effort. In exchange, they charge commission fees based on the sale price. The trade-off here is the convenience and professional exposure consignment shops provide, potentially leading to higher sale prices than individual efforts might yield.

If considering this route, research local consignment shops to find one that aligns with the type of items you have for sale. Ask about their commission rates and any specific requirements or preferences for the items they accept. Once an agreement is reached, drop off your items and let the professionals do the rest, freeing you up from the day-to-day management of selling.

Estate Sales

Estate sales offer yet another perspective, especially useful when dealing with a whole household's contents. Typically managed by professionals, these sales are designed to liquidate an entire estate, making them ideal for those moving into smaller homes or needing to clear out after losing a loved one. Estate sale organizers typically handle everything from sorting and pricing to advertising and selling items, ensuring maximum exposure and revenue.

Choosing to conduct an estate sale means less personal involvement, but potentially better results due to the expertise of the organizers in pricing and promoting items efficiently. Professionals in this field know how to categorize and display items to attract serious buyers and ensure competitive pricing strategies. They also alleviate the stress of managing a large-scale sale by handling logistics and dealing with large crowds of customers.

How to Donate Effectively

Donating items when moving house can be beneficial for several reasons, as it helps reduce the number of belongings you need to pack and move, making the process easier and more organized. Donating items also allows you to give to those in need, providing them with useful items that you no longer need, promotes recycling, and reduces waste by keeping items out of landfills.

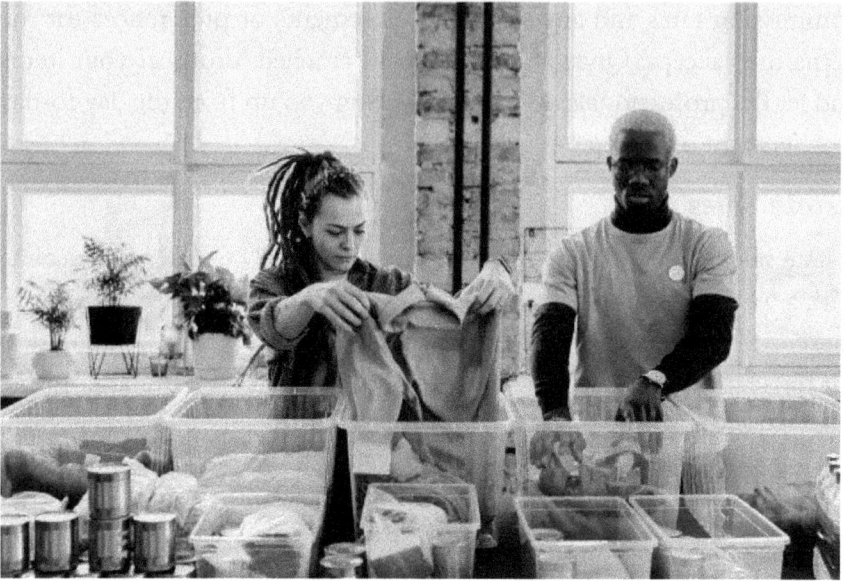

Furthermore, donations to charitable organizations may be tax-deductible, providing you with potential financial benefits. Donating fosters a sense of community and goodwill, allowing you to contribute positively to society, and can create a more spacious environment in your new home, allowing you to organize and start fresh. Fewer items mean a lighter load, which can lower moving costs and reduce the stress of relocating. Below, we look at a few strategies to help you donate effectively when decluttering and downsizing.

Do Your Research

When it comes to donating goods, the ultimate goal is to maximize their usefulness to the recipients. This starts with doing some homework on the charities you are considering. Taking the time to research these organizations helps ensure your donations go to places that best align with your personal values and also make effective use of what you provide. Not all charities operate in the same way; some have broader missions while others focus on specific needs. By knowing where your items will end up and how they'll be used, you can make informed decisions that ultimately benefit both you and the organization you choose to donate to.

A crucial step in the donation process is verifying acceptance policies. Charities and thrift stores typically have guidelines about the condition of the items they receive. Ensuring that your donated goods meet these criteria not only saves the organization's time and effort but also raises the likelihood that your items will be used effectively. Take the example of donating clothing: Nearly new pieces without holes or stains are far more likely to be accepted compared to worn-out apparel. Similarly, household items should be clean and functional, ready for immediate use or sale. This thoughtful approach respects the organization's standards and increases the usefulness of your donations (*How to donate stuff responsibly,* n.d.).

Consider Thrift Stores

After researching potential donation destinations, consider thrift stores as an excellent option for giving away items like clothing and household goods. Thrift stores play a dual role by providing affordable shopping opportunities for community members while simultaneously raising funds for various programs. The items you donate to these stores could be resold at low prices, yet they generate significant community support. Whether it's funding youth activities, supporting shelters, or running food banks, the proceeds from thrift store sales often go back into local initiatives. It's a win-win situation: the donor clears out items they no longer need, and the thrift store converts those items into valuable resources.

While thrift stores generally accept a wide range of items, there are other organizations with more specific requirements. For example, shelters may particularly benefit from donations such as blankets, personal care products, or nonperishable food items. These types of donations directly assist individuals who rely on their services. By fulfilling these targeted needs, you contribute essential resources that support vulnerable populations. Before making a trip to drop off your contributions, contact the shelter to understand their current needs. This saves you the hassle of transporting unwanted items and ensures your donation makes a meaningful impact.

In addition to checking item conditions, pay attention to seasonal demands and special notices posted by donation sites. Many thrift stores display signs indicating which items they are currently accepting or have enough of. Donating winter coats in the dead of summer, for example, may not be as useful as waiting until colder months when demand peaks. Respecting these logistical considerations optimizes the value of your contribution. Moreover, arranging your items neatly before handing them over can be incredibly helpful. Simple acts like bagging small accessories together or labeling ambiguous items take little effort on your part but save volunteers enormous time and energy during the sorting process (*How to donate stuff responsibly*, n.d.).

Make a Cash Donation

Sometimes the best donations are not materials at all but monetary contributions derived from the sale of your goods. Selling your items and donating the proceeds to charity gives these organizations greater flexibility in addressing immediate needs. Local yard sales or online platforms can help you sell items efficiently, and you can choose to support any cause you wish with the income. What's more, direct financial support often has a much broader impact than physical items, allowing charities to allocate funds where they're most effective.

Recycling and Responsible Disposal

Recycling is something we all know we should do, but how often do we stop to think about what materials can go into that blue bin? Let's break it down to make sure we're doing our part efficiently, and why it's important.

It's key to identify what your local recycling program accepts; common recyclables include plastics, metals, and paper products.

- **Plastics** are a bit tricky because not all types are the same. Check the recycling symbols on containers—numbers 1 (PETE) and 2 (HDPE) are generally accepted almost everywhere, but you might struggle with others like number 4 (LDPE) or number 5 (PP), depending on your local facilities.

- **Metals** such as aluminum cans and tin cans are widely recyclable. Paper products, including newspapers, mixed papers, and cardboard, are also usually good to go.

- Remember that **contamination** is a big problem: Food or liquid residues can spoil whole batches. So, rinsing out those peanut butter jars or soup cans before recycling makes a huge difference.

Upcycling

- Beyond traditional recycling, there's an exciting movement toward reshaping the lifecycle of goods. It's called upcycling, and it transforms old items into new treasures. This isn't just for the crafty among us; anyone can get involved! Consider repurposing glass jars as storage solutions, using wooden pallets to build garden furniture, or transforming old clothes into creative quilts. Here are some examples of upcycling:

- **Furniture Redesign**: Transforming old wooden pallets into stylish coffee tables or chairs.

- **Glass Jar Storage**: Use glass jars as storage containers for pantry items, craft supplies, or bathroom essentials.

- **T-Shirt Tote Bags**: Converting old T-shirts into reusable tote bags by cutting and tying the fabric.

- **Wine Cork Crafts**: Making coasters, bulletin boards, or trivets from used wine corks.

- **Tin Can Planters**: Repurposing empty tin cans as plant pots by painting them and creating drainage holes.

- **Drawer Shelves**: Turning old drawers into wall-mounted shelves for decorative storage.

- **Spoon Hooks**: Bending old spoons to create unique hooks for hanging keys or jewelry.

- **Book Page Art**: Using pages from old books to create wall art, garlands, or decorative origami.

- **Old Jeans Pouches**: Sewing old jeans into small pouches or organizers for tools or stationery.

- **Furniture Upholstery**: Reupholstering old chairs or sofas with new fabric to give them a fresh look.

Upcycling not only reduces waste but can also save money and provide a unique charm to your home that store-bought items simply can't compete with. What are you waiting for? Start upcycling today!

Dealing With Hazardous Materials

Recycling hazardous materials involves the proper collection, treatment, and recycling of substances that can pose risks to human health or the environment. Here are key points about recycling hazardous materials:

1. **Types of Hazardous Materials**: Common hazardous materials include batteries, electronics, paint, chemicals, pesticides, lights (fluorescent bulbs), and certain medical waste.

2. **Environmental Protection**: Recycling hazardous materials helps prevent pollution, reduces landfill waste, and ensures that harmful substances are managed safely.

3. **Specialized Facilities**: Hazardous materials should be taken to specialized recycling facilities equipped to handle and process them safely. These facilities follow strict regulations to minimize risks.

4. **Community Programs**: Many communities offer recycling programs or events for hazardous materials, making it easier for residents to dispose of these items responsibly.

5. **Proper Disposal**: Never throw hazardous materials in regular trash or down the drain. Proper disposal and recycling help avoid contamination of soil and water sources.

6. **Health Risks**: Improper handling of hazardous materials can lead to health issues, including respiratory problems, skin irritation, or even more severe chronic conditions.

7. **Regulatory Compliance**: Many countries have regulations governing the disposal and recycling of hazardous materials to protect public health and the environment.

8. **Awareness**: Educating the public about the importance of recycling hazardous materials can lead to better compliance and safer communities.

Recycling hazardous materials contributes to a safer ecosystem and promotes sustainable practices.

Handling hazardous materials requires caution. Items like batteries, paint, motor oil, and chemicals pose significant risks if disposed of improperly. Municipal guidelines often dictate the safe handling of these materials. For instance, used batteries can leach toxic metals into soil and water if thrown in with regular trash. Fortunately, many stores and service stations offer battery and oil recycling programs. It's also not uncommon to find community hazardous waste collection days dedicated to these types of disposal, ensuring they're safely processed. Following these protocols isn't just good sense—it's crucial for preventing harm to both human health and the environment.

Getting Rid of Items with Special Disposal Requirements

How do you recycle hard-to-handle items like electronics or large appliances? These don't belong in your curbside bins but need special care. Why? They often contain valuable resources and hazardous components. By locating specialized centers for electronic waste, you ensure that these items are dismantled properly, allowing their parts to be recycled without environmental damage. Many communities host regular e-waste collection events or have designated drop-off points for these items. It might take a bit more effort, but it significantly reduces harmful waste in landfills.

Recycling electronics and large appliances involves a few important steps to ensure they are disposed of safely and responsibly. Here's how to do it:

1. **Check Local Regulations**: Research your local recycling laws and guidelines, as they can vary by area. Some regions have specific rules for electronic and appliance disposal.

2. **Find Certified E-Waste Recyclers**: Look for certified e-waste recycling centers that specialize in recycling electronics. These facilities are equipped to handle hazardous materials often found in electronics safely.

3. **Community Collection Events**: Many communities host e-waste collection events where you can drop off unwanted electronics and large appliances for recycling.

4. **Manufacturer Take-Back Programs**: Some manufacturers offer take-back programs that allow you to return old electronics or appliances for recycling. Check the manufacturer's website for details.

5. **Donation Options**: If the electronics or appliances are still functional, consider donating them to charities, schools, or community organizations that can reuse them.

6. **Remove Personal Data**: Before recycling electronics, ensure that you remove personal data by factory resetting devices or using data-wiping software.

7. **Proper Disposal of Batteries**: If your electronics contain batteries, remove them and recycle them separately at designated battery recycling locations.

8. **Check for Bulk Waste Pickup**: Some waste management services offer bulk waste pickup for large appliances. Schedule a pickup if available in your area.

9. **Follow Guidelines**: When dropping off items for recycling, follow the recycler's guidelines for what materials they accept to ensure proper processing.

10. **Keep It Separate**: Store electronics and appliances separately from regular trash to avoid contamination and promote responsible disposal.

By following these steps, you can help ensure that electronics and large appliances are recycled properly, reducing environmental impact and promoting sustainability.

Disposal of Larger Items

When you have a big clear-out, you usually have to get rid of items that won't fit in the garbage bin. Here are some effective ways to dispose of household items that won't fit in the regular garbage bin:

- **Bulk Waste Pickup**: Many municipalities have bulk waste collection days or special programs for large items like furniture and mattresses. Contact your local waste management service for details.

- **Freecycle**: Use platforms like Freecycle, where you can give away items for free to people in your community.

- **Storage Units**: If you don't want to part with certain items but need to get them out of your home, consider renting a storage unit temporarily.

- **Curbside Giveaway**: If local regulations allow, place items you want to give away on the curb with a "free" sign. Many people will pick them up.

- **Donation Pickups**: Some charities may also schedule pickup appointments for larger items, so check if any local organizations offer this service.

- **Landfill or Transfer Station**: As a last resort, you can take items to a landfill or transfer station, but make sure to check what items are accepted.

- **Hire a Skip**: You can hire a skip to dispose of larger items or large amounts of waste generated by a move. Arrange to have it picked up by the company you hired it from when it is full.

Benefits of Giving Items a New Life and Supporting Those in Need

For those considering downsizing, perhaps due to retirement or other lifestyle changes, understanding these practices becomes particularly relevant. Not only will it make letting go of items easier, knowing they're being reused or broken down responsibly, but it will contribute to a sustainable future for all. Downsizing doesn't mean discarding everything blindly. Rather, it offers the opportunity to contribute positively to the world around us, turning potential clutter into components of a cleaner, healthier planet.

Living in alignment with these principles helps everyone participate in a wider, collective social effort. From the perspective of adult lives transitioning through phases, there's a sense of giving back to the Earth that has sustained us. Downsizing can feel liberating if it's handled thoughtfully and with an eco-conscious approach. These practices, when imbued with personal commitment and mindfulness, ripple through communities, creating positive change that extends far beyond one household's confines.

Summary

Here we have explored practical ways to approach letting go of items while being mindful of their next destination. Whether you're looking to sell, donate, or recycle, the key is finding the method that resonates with your lifestyle and values. Selling can be a rewarding venture, offering both financial benefits and a sense of accomplishment as you see unwanted goods finding new homes. Meanwhile, donating gives your items a second life and helps those in need, either by supporting local charities or specific individuals who could benefit from them. Recycling ensures we're doing our part for the planet, reducing waste and conserving resources for future generations. By carefully considering each item and its possibilities, you not only create space in your home but also contribute positively to your community and the environment.

As you navigate these options, it's important to balance practicality with empathy, recognizing that downsizing is more than just a physical decluttering—it's an emotional process, too. By thoughtfully choosing what to keep and what to let go, you honor your past while embracing a future filled with potential and simplicity. Remember, each decision contributes to a broader narrative of sustainability and generosity, not just shaping your living space but also leaving a lasting impact on those around you.

Chapter 6

Downsizing With Seniors – Special Considerations

Downsizing with seniors involves more than just reducing the number of belongings; it's a sensitive journey that requires understanding and patience. Recognizing the emotional ties older people have to their homes and possessions is crucial, as these items often represent cherished memories and personal achievements. This transition can be overwhelming, so approaching conversations with empathy and active listening is vital. By validating their feelings and showing genuine interest in their experiences, we can encourage trust and ease anxieties around this significant life change. It's about walking alongside them, respecting their pace, and ensuring they feel supported every step of the way.

Below, we dive into various strategies to support seniors during the downsizing process, emphasizing the importance of empathetic communication and a gradual introduction to the concept. By illustrating different housing options and taking a collaborative approach, we aim to make the transition smoother and more respectful, ensuring that seniors maintain a sense of control over their own lives.

Approaching the Topic of Downsizing with Older Family Members

When it comes to downsizing with seniors, facilitating open conversations is crucial. First and foremost, introducing guidelines when discussing downsizing with older family members can prevent misunderstandings and ease tension. Approach the topic gently, ensuring it's a two-way dialogue rather than a directive. Set aside dedicated times for these conversations, free from distractions, making sure each party feels comfortable voicing their thoughts and feelings. Respectful dialogue fosters collaboration and mutual respect, laying a foundation for productive decision-making.

Throughout the process, remain patient and flexible. Understand that every individual processes change at their own pace, and rushing decisions might lead to regret or dissatisfaction later on. Offer small steps to break the process into manageable tasks, such as starting with decluttering less sentimental areas before tackling rooms filled with cherished items. Celebrating each step of the journey helps build momentum and confidence, making the entire undertaking seem less daunting.

The process can be emotionally and practically challenging for everyone involved, but approaching these discussions with empathy and active listening can help ease the transition. It's important to understand that many seniors may have deep connections to their homes and belongings. These attachments are tied to memories, significant life events, and personal achievements. Listening actively means not only hearing words but also paying attention to emotions and nonverbal cues. This level of attentiveness helps you truly understand their concerns and assists in providing the emotional support they need.

Below, we give some important pointers for broaching the topic of downsizing with older adults.

Be Empathetic

Empathy is key. Put yourself in the shoes of your older friends and family; consider what it might feel like to part with items accumulated over a lifetime or to leave a home where countless memories were made. Acknowledge their feelings and validate their experiences so they feel heard and supported. For example, instead of saying "It's just stuff," try expressing understanding by sharing sentiments like, "I can't imagine how hard this must be for you to decide what stays and what goes." Words matter and showing that you care about their experiences can go a long way in building trust and easing anxiety.

Introduce the Topic Gradually

Introducing the topic of downsizing gradually is another effective strategy. Sudden changes can often lead to resistance, as they can be overwhelming. Begin by casually discussing the benefits of downsizing during relaxed moments, perhaps when reminiscing about past adventures or considering future ones. For instance, while flipping through old travel photos, you might gently bring up how a simpler space could mean more freedom to explore new destinations without worrying about maintaining a large home. This approach allows them time to digest the idea, envision new possibilities, and eventually embrace the change without feeling pressured.

Highlight the Benefits of Downsizing

Highlighting the benefits of downsizing can naturally encourage a positive outlook. Reduced upkeep is one of the most appealing aspects, as smaller spaces typically require less cleaning, fewer repairs, and lower utility costs. Many seniors find the financial flexibility gained from selling a larger home to be liberating, freeing up more resources to spend on activities they love or investing in their future well-being. For example, savings from reduced utility bills and maintenance costs can be redirected toward hobbies, travel, or even pampering.

Talking about the improvements in lifestyle and housing options can also spark meaningful dialogues. Encourage discussions on what kind of living arrangements would best suit their current needs and future aspirations. Ask questions like, "Do you see yourself living closer to family or in a community surrounded by peers?" or "What features are most important to you in your next home?" These inquiries invite them to dream about their ideal environment, considering factors such as accessibility, social opportunities, and amenities that enhance their quality of life.

Discussing potential lifestyle changes involves considering various elements, including healthcare proximity, social connections, and recreational activities. Transitioning to a community setting might offer access to shared resources, regular social engagements, or fitness facilities. Each option presents different advantages and should align with their personal preferences and lifestyle goals. Presenting ideas without bias encourages open-mindedness and invites seniors to feel empowered about their choices.

Use Personal Anecdotes

Conversations about downsizing might also reveal concerns about leaving familiar neighborhoods, detaching from community ties, or parting with beloved possessions. Express understanding and provide reassurance by sharing stories of others who have successfully transitioned and now enjoy a fulfilling lifestyle in their new environment. Personal anecdotes humanize the experience and show that while change can be daunting, it can also lead to rewarding outcomes.

For instance, I might relate to a senior citizen looking to downsize with the following personal anecdote:

After living in the same cozy home for over 40 years, my grandmother decided it was time to downsize. The big old house, once filled with laughter from family gatherings and the pitter-patter of my footsteps as a child, felt overwhelming for her now. As she packed up her life, memories flooded back with each item she uncovered.

One evening, as the sun set, she came across an old, dusty photo album. We spent hours together, laughing and reminiscing about family trips, birthdays, and holidays. She shared stories of how she and my grandfather had transformed the living room into a dance floor for their anniversary parties.

With every box she filled, she felt a mix of sadness and relief. She was letting go of the physical space but holding on to the memories. When the move day finally arrived, the new apartment felt fresh and vibrant, filled with just the essentials. However, the most cherished items, like her rocking chair and that photo album, found a special place in her new home.

Watching her adapt to the new environment was inspiring. My grandmother embraced this change with grace, proving that home is not just a place but the love and memories we carry with us.

Navigating Emotional Attachments and Preserving Cherished Memories

In the process of downsizing, particularly with seniors who have accumulated a lifetime of belongings, it's crucial to address the emotional aspects involved in moving house and having a clear-out and to honor cherished memories. Downsizing can be emotionally challenging, as it involves parting with possessions laden with memories and significance. To navigate this journey thoughtfully, focus on highlighting meaningful items and exploring innovative ways to preserve them.

Identify Items with Significant Social Value

Identifying items with significant sentimental value is essential. Begin by encouraging seniors to pinpoint possessions that hold special meaning. These can range from heirlooms passed down from generation to generation to everyday items that embody precious memories. Engaging seniors in conversations about the history and importance of these items can be therapeutic and grounding. This way, instead of seeing downsizing as mere decluttering, it becomes a celebration of their legacy.

Involving seniors in the decision-making process helps empower them during the transition. When they play an active role in deciding what to keep, repurpose, or donate, it respects their autonomy and supports emotional well-being. After all, downsizing isn't merely a logistical exercise; it's an emotional one that requires sensitivity and empathy.

Hold Memory-Sharing Sessions

One creative approach to preserving memories is through memory-sharing sessions. Organize gatherings where family members and friends come together to share stories associated with specific possessions. Sharing stories not only acknowledges the past but also strengthens familial bonds and brings moments of joy. These shared narratives can provide seniors with a sense of belonging and continuity, reminding them that their life stories are appreciated and cherished by those around them.

Another way of sharing memories and keeping them alive is through creating a memory box. Selecting a modest-sized memory box provides an opportunity to keep a few treasured items physically close. This could include jewelry, medals, or favorite photos. Encouraging seniors to curate a small collection of memorable items allows them to retain tangible links to their past while adhering to the practical constraints of a smaller living area. It encourages a sense of security and continuity, knowing that their most beloved possessions remain within reach.

Document Memories

Documenting memories through photographs or video recordings offers another meaningful way to capture the essence of cherished items. Encourage seniors to take photos of significant objects before letting go of them. These images can be organized into digital albums or printed and compiled into scrapbooks. For a more dynamic option, consider creating video recordings where seniors recount the stories behind the items. Not only does this preserve the memory visually, but it also captures the voice and emotions, offering a richer, multidimensional keepsake for future generations.

Moreover, using modern technology to create digital displays is a wonderful method for keeping memories alive without occupying physical space. Digital picture frames can display slideshows of scanned photographs and documents. This continuous presentation of memories can bring daily joy and reflection, seamlessly integrating the past into the present. Similarly, creating digital archives for letters and photographs protects against deterioration and facilitates easy sharing among family members.

Another technique is crafting wall collages that combine photos, small mementos, and other artifacts. Displayed prominently in the new living space, these collages serve as visual memoirs, allowing seniors to reminisce whenever they wish while adding a personal touch to the decor. It transforms the walls into a gallery of life stories and achievements, making the new environment feel homier and more familiar.

Focus on the Main Goal

Above all, the goal is to ensure that the process is seen as an opportunity rather than a loss. By focusing on preserving memories, celebrating histories, and finding new homes for well-loved items, downsizing becomes a meaningful journey of honoring the past while embracing the future. Provide reassurance and support, emphasizing that although the physical space may diminish, the richness of their life's stories and experiences remain ever-present.

Involving and Empowering Seniors in the Decision-Making Process

Involving seniors in planning and selecting their new living arrangements is a vital step in empowering them during the downsizing process. It helps ensure that they feel a sense of control over this significant life transition. Below, we look at techniques you can use to make older people feel included in the decisions connected to the downsizing process.

Discuss Preferences

Start by discussing preferences openly. This means considering what type of environment they feel most comfortable in, whether it's a smaller home, an apartment, or various senior living communities. When seniors have a say in where they will live, it can ease the anxiety associated with moving and facilitate a smoother transition. Perhaps a senior has always dreamed of living near the sea, or maybe they prefer a place within walking distance of local amenities. Taking these desires into account not only respects their wishes but also keeps them engaged and invested in the process.

Respect Individual Autonomy

Respecting autonomy is another critical aspect. Offering choices allows seniors to maintain independence, reinforcing the idea that downsizing doesn't mean losing control over their lives. Present different scenarios, such as the option between an urban setting or a quieter rural one. Respect goes beyond just offering options; it's about listening actively to their choices and incorporating those preferences into actionable plans. This approach aligns with the principles of maintaining dignity, where seniors feel empowered rather than managed. It's important to emphasize that every decision is theirs to make, and while guidance will be provided, the choice rests with them.

Adopt a Collaborative Approach

Establishing a collaborative approach can play a significant role in supporting seniors. Involve trusted family members or advisors if the senior finds value in their input. Their participation should be supportive rather than directive, ensuring that the senior remains at the center of decision-making. Trusted family members and friends can lend practical assistance and emotional support throughout the process. Additionally, geriatric care managers or social workers can bring valuable expertise to the table, helping to navigate complex choices related to health and lifestyle needs (*Family matters: How assisted living can support your loved one*, 2024). The aim here is to create a balanced team, where everyone works together respectfully, guiding without overshadowing the senior's voice.

Throughout this journey, it's crucial to remain empathetic. Downsizing is not solely about reducing square footage; it's a deeply personal process involving emotions and memories. Keeping communication open and encouraging honest dialogue about their fears and hopes will build trust.

For instance, you might suggest regular family meetings where concerns are voiced and addressed collectively. This interaction reinforces that their opinions matter and that they're not navigating this change alone.

Foster Confidence

Fostering confidence among seniors is essential, particularly by emphasizing that their input is both valuable and will be respected. Affirming their decisions by acknowledging their wisdom and experience can go a long way. Highlight past instances where their choices led to successful outcomes, reminding them of their capability to handle new situations. Use language that empowers, offering reassurance that their insights are instrumental to the success of this transition. Remember that for many seniors, the act of giving up items accumulated over a lifetime could make them feel overwhelmed. Here, providing a guideline on how to keep the process positive and respectful can help avoid feelings of being rushed or pressured. One recommendation might include setting a comfortable timeline that allows seniors to reflect and make decisions at their own pace.

Keeping the Downsizing Process Positive and Respectful

Here are some tips to ensure that seniors don't feel rushed or overwhelmed during the downsizing process:

- **Go at Their Pace**: Allow seniors to take their time with each decision and avoid rushing them.

- **Set a Comfortable Schedule**: Create a flexible timeline that accommodates breaks and allows for a relaxed pace.

- **Break Tasks Into Small Steps**: Divide the downsizing process into manageable tasks to reduce feelings of being overwhelmed.

- **Provide Emotional Support**: Acknowledge their feelings and provide reassurance throughout the process.

- **Encourage Participation in Decision-Making**: Involve seniors in decisions about what to keep or let go, giving them a sense of control.

- **Use Visual Aids**: Create checklists or charts to help visualize the downsizing steps and progress.

- **Offer Help From Family and Friends**: Encourage loved ones to lend a hand or simply provide companionship during the process.

- **Create a Comfortable Environment**: Set up an inviting space for sorting through belongings, with refreshments and seating.

- **Discuss the Benefits**: Focus on the positive aspects of moving to a new space and how it can enhance their lifestyle.

- **Celebrate Milestones**: Acknowledge and celebrate completed tasks to motivate and encourage a sense of accomplishment.

Summary

Downsizing with seniors isn't just about reducing the number of possessions or moving to a smaller home; it's a heartfelt journey filled with memories and emotions. We have explored how important it is to approach these discussions with empathy and patience. By listening actively and acknowledging their feelings, you're not only helping them part with treasured belongings and transition to a better living environment but are also providing essential emotional support. Talking about the benefits of downsizing gradually encourages acceptance and allows your loved ones to see the exciting possibilities ahead. Whether it's simplifying their lifestyle or exploring new adventures, the process should always be about empowering them to make decisions that respect their wishes and aspirations.

Involving seniors in the decision-making process fosters confidence and maintains their independence during this significant life transition. Discussing preferences for new living arrangements ensures they feel in control and valued. It's about creating a supportive environment where choices are respected, and transitions are made at a comfortable pace. By working together—whether with family, friends, or professionals—you can transform downsizing from a daunting task into an enriching experience. Remember, the key is patience, understanding, and open dialogue to make sure every step honors their past while embracing the future with optimism and hope.

Chapter 7

Moving Day and Settling into Your New Home

Moving day is an experience many have faced, yet it is a day that is often dreaded. The prospect often mingles excitement with a healthy dose of stress. Moving isn't just about physically transporting belongings from one place to another; it's an emotional and life-altering event that can redefine your sense of home and personal space. It's a chance to evaluate what you truly need and want in your life as you step into a new chapter. However, the process, if well-planned and organized, can be transformed into an empowering transition rather than a daunting challenge.

Below, we'll guide you through every step of preparing for your big move, ensuring a smooth and efficient process.

Preparing for the Big Day

Moving day can be a daunting prospect, especially when balancing the emotional weight of transitioning and the physical demands of moving. But with some guidance and organization, you can make this process more efficient and even enjoyable. Here, we explore how to streamline your packing and moving preparation, ensuring everything is in place to help ease the transition into your new home.

Create a Room-by-Room Checklist

Organizing your belongings using a room-by-room checklist is essential. This method ensures that nothing gets overlooked in the chaos of moving. Here's a step-by-step guide to creating a room-by-room checklist for moving house:

1. **Gather Supplies**: Get notebooks, pens, or digital devices where you can document your checklist.

2. **Create a Template**: Make categories for each room in your house (e.g., living room, kitchen, bedrooms, bathrooms, garage).

3. **List Items Room by Room**:

   - **Living Room**: sofas, chairs, coffee table, TV, bookshelves, decorations

   - **Kitchen**: appliances, utensils, pots, pans, dishes, food items

   - **Bedrooms**: beds, dressers, nightstands, clothes, accessories

   - **Bathrooms**: toiletries, towels, shower curtains, rugs

   - **Garage/Storage**: tools, outdoor equipment, seasonal items

4. **Decide on Moving Methods**: Note how you will move larger items (hiring movers, renting a truck, etc.).

5. **Labeling**: Create a labeling system for boxes that specify the room they belong to and brief contents.

6. **Cleaning**: Add tasks for cleaning each room before and after packing.

7. **Utilities**: Remember to note down utility cancellations, transfers, or setups for the new house.

8. **Final Checks**: Include a section for last-minute checks to ensure nothing is forgotten, such as checking closets, drawers, and under furniture.

9. **Schedule Timeline**: Add deadlines for each room's packing to keep yourself on track.

10. **Review and Adjust**: As you progress, update and adjust the checklist as needed.

Having a detailed checklist will help make your move organized and efficient. Begin with rooms that have items you seldom use. These could be guest rooms or storage areas. Packing these early will reduce anxiety about last-minute tasks. Create a list for each room, noting essentials and those items you can do without immediately.

Remember, no item is too small to deserve attention. Is the spare charger tucked away in a drawer? It might prove invaluable once you're settled into your new abode. These seemingly minor details contribute significantly to a smooth transition.

Utilize Effective Packing Techniques

When packing, effective techniques are vital. The goal is to protect your valuables while also maximizing space. It starts with acquiring a variety of box sizes suitable for different items around your home. Use strong adhesive tape to seal boxes and secure bubble wrap around fragile items, ensuring their safety during transit (How to Pack for a Move: A Checklist by Room, n.d.). For smaller, easily misplaced items like silverware, plastic bags can be invaluable. Don't overlook the utility knife or scissors; having tools on hand makes cutting packing materials seamless, reducing frustration.

Packing techniques matter greatly when safeguarding items. For instance, wrapping delicate kitchenware with bubble wrap or newspaper offers an extra layer of protection against shocks and movement during transport. Blankets can serve as padding for larger fragile items such as mirrors or furniture. If you're storing items long term, choosing waterproof containers helps keep them safe from moisture damage. Similar care should be taken for electronic devices. Photograph their setups before dismantling cables. Keeping photos handy aids in reconstructing configurations without hassle. Also, color-coding wires pay dividends in reassembly, helping distinguish between a mess of cables and cords.

Maximize the space within each box wisely. Heavy items should sit at the bottom, with lighter ones stacked above, preventing structural damage to the contents. Filling every crevice with softer materials like towels or biodegradable packing peanuts can further cushion and protect valuables (*How to pack for a move: Room by room checklist*, 2024). Remember, the more efficiently you pack, the fewer boxes you'll need, saving both space and money.

Label

Labeling is another crucial aspect of packing. Use permanent markers to denote what each box contains and which room it belongs to.

This step is more than just about knowing what's inside; it directly impacts the efficiency of unpacking. Consider adding color codes for easy identification, especially if using a mover service where many eyes and hands are involved. A well-labeled box translates to an organized move-in day.

Having a plan for documentation and essential supplies is nonnegotiable. On moving day, having a "day-of" box filled with necessities can prevent undue stress. This box might include essential documents—such as contracts, IDs, or important financial papers—and basic supplies like toiletries and snacks for the new home. Keep this box in an accessible spot so it's the first thing you unpack, allowing you to handle any immediate needs upon arrival.

Complete All Important Paperwork

Compiling all critical paperwork and having it handy ensures you aren't turning your home upside down later to find that one elusive form. Before moving house, make sure to have the following important paperwork completed:

- **Rental or Sale Agreement**: Ensure you have a signed lease or sales contract for the new property.

- **Change of Address Form**: Complete this form with the postal service to forward your mail.

- **Utility Transfers**: Prepare paperwork for transferring or setting up utilities like electricity, water, gas, internet, and cable.

- **Insurance Documents**: Review and update your home insurance policy for the new address.

- **Inventory List**: Create an inventory of your belongings, especially if you're moving valuable items.

- **Moving Company Agreement**: If hiring movers, have a formal agreement detailing services and costs.

- **Permission and Access Forms**: If applicable, get permission forms for any community or association rules that need to be followed.

- **School Records**: If you have children, ensure their school records are transferred to their new schools.

- **Medical Records**: Obtain copies of medical records if you're changing healthcare providers.

- **Financial Documents**: Keep copies of important financial documents, such as mortgage documents, closing statements, and tax information.

Having these documents in order will help facilitate a smoother transition to your new home. A binder or folder categorizing these documents can be a lifesaver.

Set Realistic Timelines

As moving day approaches, try setting realistic timelines. Allow plenty of time for each stage, from initial organization to final clean-up at your old home. Rushing often leads to mistakes or forgotten items. Creating a general schedule and sticking to it keeps momentum going and reduces stress levels.

Below, we present an example of a timeline for moving house, broken down into key phases from initial organization to the final clean-up:

8 Weeks Before Moving

- **Start Organizing**: Create a moving binder to keep track of all moving-related paperwork.

- **Research Moving Companies**: Request quotes and schedule movers if needed.

6 Weeks Before Moving

- **Notify Landlord or Real Estate Agent**: If renting, give notice. If selling, finalize the sale agreement.

- **Begin Packing Nonessentials**: Pack items you won't need until after the move (seasonal clothing, decor, etc.).

- **Change of Address**: Fill out the change of address form at the post office.

4 Weeks Before Moving

- **Finalize Utility Transfers**: Schedule disconnection at your old home and connection at the new one.

- **Pack Room by Room**: Start packing by room, labeling boxes with their contents and destination rooms.

- **Notify Important Contacts**: Inform friends, family, and relevant services (banks, subscriptions) of your new address.

2 Weeks Before Moving

- **Confirm Details with Movers**: Confirm dates, services, and any special instructions.

- **Pack Essential Items**: Prepare an essentials box with things you'll need on moving day (clothes, toiletries, important documents).

- **Prepare for Pets/Plants**: Make arrangements for moving pets or plants.

1 Week Before Moving

- **Finalize Packing**: Aim to have everything packed, except for daily essentials.

- **Clean the Old Home**: Do a preliminary clean-up to avoid overwhelming tasks on moving day.

- **Review Inventory List**: Check your packing list and ensure you have everything accounted for.

Moving Day

- **Last-Minute Packing**: Pack up remaining essentials/last-minute items.

- **Oversee the Move**: Ensure the movers handle your belongings with care and supervise the loading process.

- **Do a Final Walk-Through**: Check all rooms, closets, and storage areas to avoid leaving anything behind.

After the Move

- **Settle Into Your New Home**: Unpack and organize room by room, starting with essential areas like the kitchen and bedrooms.

- **Final Clean-Up of Old Home**: Once everything is moved out, do a thorough clean-up of the old home to fulfill lease or sale obligations.

- **Update Documents**: Once settled, make sure to update your address on any important documents.

This timeline or a similar one should help you stay organized and ensure a smooth moving process!

Planning for a Smooth Transition

Moving into a new home is a significant event in anyone's life, especially when you're downsizing or making lifestyle changes later in life. Ensuring that every family member, from the youngest to the furriest, experiences a smooth transition is vital for maintaining emotional and physical well-being during this period. In this section, we look at techniques you can apply to make downsizing smoother for the entire family.

Utilize Familiar Items and Routines

It's important to ensure that children and pets are prepared with familiar items and routines to reduce stress. Kids can find moving daunting, as they're leaving behind friends, schools, and familiar environments. To ease their anxieties, incorporate elements of fun and familiarity. Before the move, encourage them to pack a "special box" containing their favorite toys, books, or games that will travel with them rather than with the moving truck. These items can provide comfort amid all the chaos. Furthermore, maintain a dialogue about what the moving day will entail to set proper expectations. Once you arrive at your new home, establish a space with their special items immediately available.

However, moving doesn't end once boxes are unpacked; routine plays a pivotal role in settling into a new home. Children might still have lingering feelings about the move. Encourage open conversations about their thoughts and ensure regular meals and bedtime routines are maintained.

Similarly, pets also need careful consideration. Much like children, animals thrive on routine and can become stressed by changes in their environment. Start by preparing a pet-specific travel bag filled with essentials like food, water, toys, and blankets that smell like home.

During the move, ensure they have a quiet area where they feel safe, perhaps even boarding them elsewhere to keep them away from the noise and disruption. On arrival at the new house, designate a specific area for your pet with their bed and familiar items so they can settle down quickly.

Like children, pets need to adhere to their normal routines to settle into a new environment. So, continue walking your pet at regular intervals and closely monitor how they adapt to their new home.

Set Up Basic Necessities at Your New Home

Arranging the setup of basic necessities at the new home will ease the initial adjustment for everyone. While it might be tempting to unpack all at once, prioritize areas that contribute most to comfort and functionality. Focus first on establishing the kitchen, bathrooms, and bedrooms. Having access to essential food, toiletries, and a comfortable place to sleep is vital. For your own peace of mind, ensure these spaces are organized before turning attention to lesser-used areas of the house.

Complete a Few Manageable Goals Each Day

A helpful guideline in making the transition smooth for everyone is setting a few manageable goals daily. Instead of tackling everything head-on and risking burnout, divide tasks over a week. Perhaps aim to have one common area fully set up per day, which keeps progress steady without overwhelming anyone. Encouraging family members to take breaks and explore your new neighborhood bit by bit also aids in adjusting to the new environment.

Integrate Yourself in Your New Neighborhood

Organizing an introductory gathering or participating in neighborhood events can create a welcoming atmosphere. Building connections within the local community strengthens belonging and helps establish new friendships. Create lasting memories by hosting a housewarming gathering. Inviting friends and family to share in your new beginning not only strengthens bonds but also fills your home with positive energy. As you plan your event, keep it simple and authentic. Consider a casual get-together with finger foods and beverages, allowing guests to mingle and explore different rooms at their leisure. If your circle includes individuals unfamiliar with one another, arrange interactive activities to encourage conversation and connection.

Engage your family in joint activities like decorating shared spaces or exploring nearby parks. These shared endeavors further instill a sense of adventure and renewal associated with this significant life change. Explore the local area together, participate in community events, or embark on a group project like planting a garden. Such endeavors provide opportunities to build new traditions while cementing your sense of belonging within the neighborhood. Reflecting on these shared experiences will endear your new home to you, as it becomes a repository of joyous occasions and heartfelt moments.

Unpacking Strategically

Moving to a new home can be both exciting and overwhelming, especially as you aim to establish an organized and inviting living space quickly and comfortably. To achieve this, consider unpacking strategically to set up your new space with intention, personalizing spaces, and creating warm memories by engaging in meaningful activities. This approach will help transform your new house into a welcoming haven that feels like home.

Prioritize Essential Areas

When unpacking, prioritize essential areas like the kitchen and bedrooms. Your kitchen is the heart of your home, where daily activities such as cooking and dining take place. Begin by organizing your kitchen essentials—unpack cookware, utensils, and pantry items first. Arrange them efficiently to suit your daily routines. A well-organized kitchen will allow you to settle in comfortably, letting you enjoy your first meals without unnecessary stress. Similarly, setting up the bedrooms should be a priority. Ensure beds are assembled and dressed with clean linens, offering everyone a cozy night's rest after a long day of moving. Unpacking essentials like clothes and toiletries will further contribute to a sense of normalcy.

Personalize Your New Home

To truly make the space yours, personalize it with decorations and arrangements that reflect your family's identity. Display family photos, cherished art pieces, or travel mementos that bring joy and comfort. These personal touches transform bland walls into memory-laden canvases, providing a visual reminder of who you are and what you value. It's important to select decorations that speak to your collective story, ensuring each room resonates with familiarity and warmth. An added benefit is the opportunity for creativity—experiment with colors and layouts to create a unique ambiance tailored to your preferences.

Natural elements can significantly enhance your home's atmosphere. Consider incorporating plants and flowers, which not only add beauty but also improve air quality. Choose easy-to-care-for greenery, like succulents or ferns, if you're new to plant care, or indulge in more vibrant blooms if gardening is already a passion. The presence of nature within your home injects life into spaces, making them feel cozier and more inviting. Additionally, use natural materials, such as wooden furniture or stone accents, to bring texture and warmth, grounding your environment with earthy tones.

Lighting plays a crucial role in setting the mood of your home. Opt for warm-colored light bulbs to make your space feel inviting. Use a mix of overhead lighting and softer sources like table lamps or floor lamps to create a balance. This combination allows for flexibility, enabling you to adjust the lighting to suit various activities, be it relaxing with a book or hosting a dinner party. Incorporating dimmers provides an extra layer of control, allowing you to tailor the ambiance to your liking effortlessly.

In essence, establishing an organized and inviting living space quickly and comfortably involves a thoughtful blend of prioritization and personalization. By unpacking strategically, you lay the groundwork for seamless daily routines. Personalizing your space with decorative elements ensures every corner exudes warmth and familiarity.

Reflecting on the Moving Journey and Celebrating Your Accomplishments

Once you have moved into your new property, you will want to relax and celebrate. Reflecting on your moving journey and celebrating its completion can be a rewarding experience. Here's how you can do it:

- **Take Time to Reflect**: Set aside some quiet time to think about the entire moving process. Consider what went well, what challenges you faced, and how you overcame them.

- **Journal Your Experiences**: Write down your thoughts and feelings about the move, including any memorable moments, lessons learned, and changes you'd make for future moves.

- **Create a Photo Album**: Compile photos from your old home, the moving process, and your new space. This visual documentation can serve as a keepsake that captures your journey.

- **Set Up a Celebration**: Host a small gathering with family or friends in your new home. This can be a housewarming party or a simple get-together to share your excitement.

- **Enjoy a Personal Treat**: Celebrate with something special for yourself, whether it's ordering your favorite meal, treating yourself to a spa day, or enjoying a fun outing.

- **Express Gratitude**: Thank those who helped you during the move, whether friends, family, or hired help. A heartfelt note or small gift can go a long way in showing appreciation.

- **Create a Vision for Your New Space**: Spend some time envisioning how you want to decorate and personalize your new home. This can be a fun way to look forward to new beginnings.

- **Set New Goals**: Establish some goals for your life in your new home, such as exploring the neighborhood, meeting new people, or starting new hobbies.

- **Plan a Relaxation Day**: After the hustle and bustle of moving, schedule a day to relax and enjoy your new surroundings, whether it's a walk in the neighborhood or a cozy day at home.

- **Reflect on Growth**: Acknowledge how far you've come and the personal growth you've experienced through the journey. Consider writing a letter to yourself to read in the future.

Taking the time to reflect and celebrate will help you process the transition and embrace the new chapter in your life!

Summary

Settling into a new home can feel like an overwhelming task, but with some careful planning and organization, it becomes an exciting step toward crafting a space that's truly yours. Creating checklists for each room and prioritizing essential areas like the kitchen and bedrooms can ease the moving process. By understanding how to efficiently pack your belongings, label boxes, and set up your new home, you can transition smoothly without losing your calm. Keeping items you need daily and essential documents accessible ensures that crucial needs are met, reducing stress for every family member, including the family pet, during the move.

As you embrace this new chapter, remember the importance of personalizing your space to reflect your unique story. Incorporating familiar and cherished items, whether they're favorite photos, works of art, or even beloved plants, add warmth to your surroundings. Engaging in activities that create new connections within your new community can create a sense of belonging. Whether you're downsizing or making a lifestyle change later in life, the journey is all about creating a home filled with love, comfort, and memories. Here's to settling in and making your new house truly feel like home!

Chapter 8

Organizing What's Left – Making the Most of Your New Space

Making the most of your new space is all about making your new home both comfortable and functional. After moving into a new home, especially if it's smaller than what you're used to, the challenge can feel overwhelming. It's not just about fitting everything in; rather, it's about creating an environment that truly supports your lifestyle. Whether you're downsizing after your kids have left the nest or embracing a simpler life in retirement, the transition brings both opportunities and challenges. By approaching this with an open mind, you can transform your new home into a place that reflects your needs and desires without feeling overwhelmed by the process.

Here, we'll dive into strategies for optimizing each room with purpose and efficiency. Whether you're looking to host family gatherings or enjoy quiet moments to yourself, these tips are designed to help you navigate the change with ease. With thoughtful planning, you can turn your living space into a welcoming oasis.

Make the Most of Space in Your New Home

Optimizing your living space involves more than just arranging your furniture; it's about creating an environment that feels comfortable and serves your needs effectively. It's important to approach these changes gradually, allowing yourself time to live in your new space and understand what works best for you. Sometimes, practical use over time reveals additional insights that initial planning might miss. Experiment with different arrangements, and don't be afraid to move things around until it feels right. Remember, the goal is to create a living environment that supports your lifestyle, whether that includes hosting family dinners or enjoying quiet afternoons with a good book. Below, we present tips for making the most of space in your new home.

Visualize and Measure Your New Space

When you're moving into a new home, especially one that might be smaller due to downsizing or lifestyle changes, it's essential to evaluate your room dimensions and layouts before setting up your furniture. This step is crucial in ensuring you make the most out of every inch available. Taking precise measurements can help prevent future headaches of having furniture that doesn't quite fit or blocks pathways.

Consider sketching a rough layout of your new space. Visualize or use online tools to experiment with where you might place each piece of furniture before actually moving it. This kind of planning not only helps with functionality but can significantly enhance comfort too. For instance, ensuring that there's enough space between each piece of furniture allows for easy movement and creates a sense of openness. It's also beneficial for reducing clutter, as well-organized spaces tend to feel less cramped.

Favor Multifunctional Furniture

Once you've got a clear understanding of your room size and potential layouts, prioritize incorporating multifunctional furniture. In recent years, this type of furniture has become increasingly popular, and for good reason. Multifunctional pieces, like a sofa bed or an ottoman with storage, are excellent solutions for smaller homes. They serve dual purposes, providing not only additional seating but also sleeping space or hidden storage areas. For example, an ottoman can be a spot to rest your feet and also store blankets or remote controls, keeping the room tidy without sacrificing style or comfort.

Make Use of Vertical Space

Another key aspect of maximizing your living space is the efficient utilization of vertical space or bare walls. Often overlooked, vertical space offers a wealth of possibilities in terms of storage and organization.

Installing shelves or overhead storage solutions can dramatically increase your room's capacity without taking up valuable floor area. High shelves can store books, decorations, or other items you don't use daily, keeping them out of the way yet accessible. Overhead cabinets in kitchens or bathrooms can house less frequently used items but still keep them within reach. These strategies not only maximize physical space but also create visual interest by drawing the eye upward, making ceilings feel higher and rooms more expansive.

Create Separate Zones

Creating distinct zones within open-plan areas is another effective strategy for making your living space both comfortable and functional. Open-floor plans are trendy, offering a modern and airy feel. However, they can sometimes lack definition, which is where creating zones comes in handy. Using rugs, partitions, or strategic furniture placement can define different areas for specific activities—like dining, working, or relaxing—without needing walls. For example, a large rug under the dining table can visually separate it from the living area, while a bookshelf can act as a divider between work and relaxation spaces without closing off either zone completely.

Storage Solutions for Smaller Spaces

When it comes to keeping your new, smaller space organized and functional, having a solid strategy for storage is key. As life changes bring about a change in living arrangements, it's important to use every inch of space wisely, ensuring that everything has its place and is easily accessible when needed. By thoughtfully incorporating storage solution strategies designed to keep smaller spaces in order, you maintain an uncluttered lifestyle even after downsizing. Remember, it starts with evaluating what you truly need and finding innovative ways to store what's left. Embrace the process of tailoring your space to fit your needs, and you'll discover that an organized home enhances not only functionality but also your peace of mind. Here's how you can implement effective storage strategies to maintain order in your downsized home.

Chose Furniture Wisely

Incorporating under-bed storage or choosing elevated furniture is an excellent way to make the most out of your floor space. The area under a bed often goes unused, yet it's perfect for storing seasonal items or belongings you don't need every day. For instance, you might store winter clothes during the summer months in vacuum-sealed bags under the bed, which keeps them out of sight but still accessible. Similarly, elevating furniture like sofas or chairs gives you additional space for placing boxes or bins underneath without cluttering any visible areas. This approach not only declutters your living area but also helps keep less frequently used items within easy reach when you do need them.

Utilize Creative Storage Solutions

A powerful tool in the quest for organization is the use of creative storage solutions like hanging organizers, rolling carts, and stackable containers. Hanging organizers can be placed inside closets or on doors, providing extra pockets for shoes, accessories, or cleaning supplies.

Rolling carts serve as mobile storage units; they're especially handy in small kitchens or bathrooms where fixed storage might be lacking. Stackable containers, meanwhile, allow you to build up rather than spread out, making use of vertical space while keeping items neatly sorted by category.

Organize

Designing a system for your belongings means thinking about what you use most often and what can be tucked away. Items you reach for every day should be within arm's reach—think about using a turntable for spices on a kitchen counter or a basket for toiletries on a bathroom shelf. For things you use less often, consider deeper storage solutions. Maybe holiday decorations go into a well-labeled box at the back of the closet, where they won't interfere with more frequently accessed items and remain hidden, reducing clutter within the home. Creating such systems reduces the hassle of searching through piles of things to find what you need and prevents chaos from taking over your spaces.

Make Use of Affordable Options

While many high-end storage solutions exist, there are plenty of affordable alternatives that provide similar effectiveness without breaking the bank. Investing in sturdy storage options doesn't always have to mean spending big—there are durable choices that suit a range of budgets. Some tips include repurposing household items as bins, baskets, or other containers you already have for storage instead of buying new ones. Also, look for discounts or deals on storage solutions at local stores or online before making purchases. Finding the right balance between cost and quality ensures your storage solutions contribute to a clutter-free lifestyle without causing financial strain (Maletic, 2024).

Maintaining an Uncluttered Lifestyle After Downsizing

When it comes to sustaining a minimalist approach while embracing simplicity, you need to explore ways to maintain an uncluttered lifestyle after downsizing. Below, we present some tips to help you do just that!

Develop a Decluttering Routine

The journey begins with developing a consistent routine for decluttering. Regularly scheduled sessions can serve as an essential way of maintaining your new space's tranquility and order. The idea is not just to clean out a closet but to establish a habit that prevents accumulation over time. Think of this as a way to reflect on what's truly important and make conscious decisions about the things you allow into your life.

Start Small

For many, the process of decluttering may feel daunting, much like diving into an unfamiliar pool. However, by starting small—perhaps focusing on one room or even a single drawer—you create manageable tasks that won't overwhelm you. Over time, these small efforts culminate in significant change, as each session helps chip away at unnecessary clutter. This methodical approach not only makes the process less intimidating but also fosters a sense of achievement as you see spaces transform before your eyes.

Quality Over Quantity

Adopting a mindset focused on quality over quantity plays a crucial role in downsizing, decluttering, and minimalist living. It's about investing in items that add genuine value to your life and choosing durable and versatile possessions. This shift from seeking numerous transient items to valuing lasting, multifunctional ones has both emotional and financial benefits. Imagine owning a few pieces of clothing that mix and match seamlessly rather than a closet stuffed with clothes rarely worn. By opting for quality, you reduce waste, save money in the long run, and contribute to environmental sustainability (Knyszewski, 2024).

Establish Clear Criteria

Establishing clear criteria for keeping items is another pillar of decluttering. Deciding whether to keep something could be based on its function, sentimental value, or frequency of use. Functionality ensures that the items you retain serve a practical purpose in daily life. Sentimentality, meanwhile, allows space for meaningful keepsakes that hold personal history. However, balance is key; overly sentimental attachment can lead to a home filled with things that weigh you down rather than uplift you. Lastly, consider how often an item is used. If it's been gathering dust without fulfilling any meaningful role, perhaps it's time to let it go.

Incorporating Minimalist Principles

Minimalism is a lifestyle and philosophy that emphasizes living with less is important if you wish to focus on what truly matters. It involves simplifying one's life by reducing physical possessions, distractions, and excess in various areas such as home, work, and relationships. Minimalists often aim to prioritize experiences, meaningful relationships, and personal growth over the accumulation of material goods. The core idea is that by decluttering and embracing simplicity, individuals can create more space and time for what truly enriches their lives.

Mindful purchasing decisions are vital in maintaining minimalism and embracing a "less is more" mindset. Such purchasing decisions help you to develop a decluttering routine, promote quality over quantity, and establish clear criteria for keeping or discarding items.

Before acquiring a new item, ask yourself:

- Do I need this?

- Will it add value to my life?

- Is there already something I own that serves the same purpose?

These questions guide you toward more thoughtful consumption, curbing impulse buys that clutter your living space. This intentional approach becomes especially powerful when combined with the "one in, one out" rule, where for every new item brought in, an old one departs, ensuring balance within your home.

In today's fast-paced world, it's easy to fall into the trap of buying things because they are trendy or advertised as must-haves. However, by embracing minimalism, we challenge the societal pressures that equate ownership with happiness. Minimalists find joy in simplicity and freedom from the constant desire for more. It's about creating an environment where every possession has a purpose and contributes positively to your lifestyle.

Benefits of Embracing Minimalism

The rewards of such a lifestyle extend beyond physical spaces. Simplifying surroundings can lead to improved mental clarity and emotional well-being (Shaw, 2024). A decluttered home often translates to a decluttered mind, free from distractions and the stress of excess. Many find that reducing tangible clutter also leads to a more organized mental state, promoting relaxation and a sense of calm.

A common misconception is that minimalism equals deprivation. On the contrary, it's about having enough—enough to support your needs and bring joy, without the burden of excess. When you focus on simplifying, life gradually transforms, providing more room for experiences, relationships, and personal growth. This mindset allows individuals to create a deeply personalized living space that aligns with their values and aspirations.

For those who wish to embrace minimalism, patience and persistence are key. It's essential to remember that minimalism isn't a one-size-fits-all solution but a personal path shaped by individual preferences and circumstances. Take time to assess your values and explore what genuinely brings you joy. Whether through small, consistent efforts or broader lifestyle shifts, embracing minimalism can ultimately lead to richer and more fulfilling days.

Summary

Moving into a new home can feel like stepping into a fresh chapter of life, especially if downsizing has been part of the journey. Above, we explored how to make the most out of your space, ensuring it remains both functional and inviting. By planning your layout carefully, you give yourself the freedom to move easily and enjoy your surroundings. Multifunctional furniture plays a big role here, offering solutions that don't sacrifice style or comfort. Utilizing vertical space is another clever way to keep things organized without feeling cramped. Remember, defining zones in open areas can help create a purpose for each corner of your home, making it feel more organized and personal.

Decluttering is not just about having less stuff; it's about having what truly matters and suits your needs. Ongoing changes are okay—living in the space will naturally lead to tweaks as you find what works best for you. Take your time to adjust and let your home reflect who you are. The goal is to maintain an uncluttered, stress-free environment where you can relax and enjoy each moment.

Chapter 9

Navigating Emotional Hurdles and Family Dynamics

Navigating emotional hurdles and family dynamics is a journey many face when leaving behind a home they have lived in for many years or even decades. The emotional ties to a house can be profound, as it holds years of memories and experiences treasured by those who lived there. Such a move is not just about changing addresses; it's a significant shift that fundamentally alters your daily life. It's like stepping into a new chapter while holding onto the pages of the past. With this transition comes a whirlwind of feelings, some anticipated and others surprising. Each room, nook, or cranny becomes a vivid reminder of shared moments and personal milestones, making the prospect of moving on feel daunting yet inevitable. Understanding these layers of emotion is key to easing the process for everyone involved. This acknowledgment is essential in respecting the sentiments tied to one's home and preparing for what's next.

Below, we look at strategies for handling resistance from family members who may find moving particularly challenging to equip you with tools to communicate effectively, navigate disagreements respectfully, and ultimately find peace amid the chaos of moving forward.

Dealing With Resistance or Reluctance From Family Members

Moving out of a long-term home can be a deeply emotional experience, and dealing with family resistance in the process can add layers of complexity. Such resistance often stems from fear of change and sentimental attachment. Identifying these common sources of resistance is crucial to navigating this challenging phase smoothly. For many, a home isn't just a physical space; it's a repository of memories and emotional bonds. The thought of leaving can bring about anxiety and reluctance, as it signifies letting go of a cherished chapter of life. Understanding and acknowledging these feelings is the first step toward addressing them.

Fear of change is a natural human reaction, particularly in older adults who find comfort in routine and familiarity. This fear can manifest as opposition to the idea of relocating. A sentimental attachment to the family home is powerful—it's not uncommon for every room or corner to have its story or memory attached to it. Recognizing these emotions is vital in empathizing with family members who may struggle with the idea of moving. Below, we look at strategies you can employ to deal with family members who express resistance or reluctance to the idea of downsizing.

Empathetic Listening

To navigate resistance or reluctance to downsize, cultivating empathetic listening skills becomes indispensable.

Empathetic listening involves truly hearing what your family members or friends are saying, both verbally and through their actions. It's about acknowledging their fears and concerns without judgment. Here are steps to practice empathetic listening:

1. **Focus Fully**: Give the speaker your undivided attention. Put away distractions, maintain eye contact, and be present.

2. **Show That You're Listening**: Use nonverbal cues like nodding and appropriate facial expressions to convey your engagement.

3. **Reflective Listening**: Paraphrase what the speaker has said to show understanding. For example, "What I hear you saying is..."

4. **Ask Open-Ended Questions**: Encourage the speaker to elaborate by asking questions that require more than a yes or no answer.

5. **Validate Feelings**: Acknowledge the speaker's emotions by saying things like, "It's understandable that you feel this way."

6. **Avoid Judgment**: Keep an open mind and refrain from making judgments or assumptions about the speaker's thoughts or feelings.

7. **Respond Appropriately**: When it's your turn to speak, share your thoughts but keep the focus on the speaker's experience.

8. **Practice Patience**: Allow silence if needed; sometimes, the speaker may need a moment to gather their thoughts.

By following these steps, you can enhance your empathetic listening skills, fostering more meaningful and supportive conversations.

Collaborative Decision-Making

Implementing collaborative decision-making approaches is another effective strategy to handle family resistance. Instead of making unilateral decisions, involve everyone in the process. This could mean discussing potential new homes together, weighing the pros and cons of each option, and considering everyone's input before making a choice.

Here are steps to practice collaborative decision-making:

- **Define the Problem**: Identify the issue that needs to be resolved, ensuring everyone understands the context.

- **Gather Diverse Perspectives**: Invite team members or stakeholders to share their views. Encourage openness and diversity of thought.

- **Set Ground Rules**: Establish guidelines for discussion to ensure respect, active listening, and equal participation from all members.

- **Brainstorm Solutions**: Facilitate a brainstorming session where all ideas are welcome. Encourage creativity without immediate criticism.

- **Evaluate Options**: Discuss the pros and cons of each idea. Use criteria important to the group to assess potential solutions.

- **Reach a Consensus**: Aim for a decision that everyone can support. This may involve compromises, so ensure all voices are heard.

- **Document the Decision**: Record the agreed-upon solution and the rationale behind it for future reference and accountability.

- **Implement and Follow Up**: Put the decision into action and regularly check in with the group to assess progress and adapt if necessary.

By engaging in these steps, you can encourage a collaborative environment that values everyone's input and leads to more effective decision-making.

Collaborative approaches encourage shared responsibility, which can lead to more positive outcomes and reduce resistance.

Cultivate Open Dialogue

Open dialogue plays a crucial role in resolving misunderstandings and promoting familial unity. Families often operate on assumptions, leading one to believe that everyone feels the same way they do about a situation.

Here are steps to cultivate open dialogue:

Create a Safe Environment

Foster a space where individuals feel comfortable sharing their thoughts without fear of judgment or retaliation.

Creating a safe environment is often crucial when navigating and solving disagreements involving downsizing. Consider Emma and Jake's story, for instance:

Two siblings, Emma and Jake, were faced with a disagreement over their elderly parents' decision to downsize from their family home of over 30 years. Emma believed they should move into a senior living community with amenities and social activities. Jake, on the other hand, felt that their parents should remain in their beloved home, which held countless cherished memories.

Tension escalated as they debated their viewpoints, often leading to unresolved conflicts that strained their relationship. Realizing that their disputes were taking a toll on their family dynamics, Emma suggested they hold a family meeting in a neutral, safe environment—the local park where they had spent many happy childhood afternoons together.

During their meeting, they set ground rules: They would listen to each other without interruption and approach the discussion with empathy. Surrounded by the soothing sounds of nature, they shared their perspectives honestly while reflecting on their parents' needs and desires.

Emma expressed her concerns about their parents' safety and well-being in a large house. Jake shared his belief that moving would strip their parents of their autonomy and happiness. As they spoke, the park's peaceful atmosphere helped both siblings to relax and truly listen to one another.

Through open communication, they realized that their parents could benefit from a balance between the two ideas. They could look for a smaller home that still allowed independence but within a supportive community. This compromise not only resolved their dispute but also reinforced their bond as siblings.

The family later toured several properties together, ultimately finding a cozy bungalow in a vibrant neighborhood, giving their parents the space they needed while ensuring a safe and nurturing environment. The experience taught Emma and Jake the power of a safe environment for resolving conflicts, leading to collaboration and a solution that respected their parents' wishes.

Emma and Jake's story also incorporates many other steps concerning encouraging an open dialogue when disagreeing about downsizing, such as:

Encourage Active Listening

Promote attentiveness by having participants listen to understand, not just to respond. Use affirming gestures and paraphrase for clarity.

Be Respectful

Show respect for differing opinions. Acknowledge that diverse perspectives enrich discussions and promote understanding.

Ask Open-Ended Questions

Use questions that require more than a yes or no answer to encourage deeper conversation and exploration of ideas.

Avoid Dominating the Conversation

Allow everyone a chance to speak. Encourage quieter individuals to share their viewpoints.

Stay Curious

Approach discussions with a mindset of curiosity. Ask follow-up questions to delve deeper into others' perspectives.

Provide Constructive Feedback

When giving feedback, frame it positively and focus on the issue rather than the person to keep the dialogue constructive.

Follow Up

After discussions, check in with participants to keep the lines of communication open and ensure ongoing dialogue.

Share Personal Experiences

Lead by example and share your own experiences or thoughts to help others feel more comfortable opening up. This tactic helped elderly friends Harold and Margaret resolve their dispute about downsizing, as related below:

Two elderly friends, Margaret and Harold, who lived next door to one another in a small village, found themselves at odds over the issue of downsizing. Both had lived in their family homes for decades, filled with memories of good times and cherished moments. However, as they aged, the responsibilities of maintaining their homes began to weigh heavily on them.

Margaret felt it was time to move into a smaller, more manageable apartment, emphasizing the convenience it would bring. Harold, on the other hand, was deeply resistant to the idea, fearing that leaving his home meant leaving behind his past and the memories he held dear.

One sunny afternoon, the two friends met for tea at their favorite café. When Margaret brought up the topic of downsizing, Harold's defenses went up immediately. Margaret could see the tension in her friend's face, which sparked an idea in her mind.

"Harold," Margaret said gently, "why don't we share our experiences? Maybe it will help us understand each other better."

Harold hesitated but eventually agreed. Margaret started, recounting her own experience of moving when her children left for college. She described the emotional challenges she faced but emphasized how liberating it felt to declutter and simplify her life. She spoke about how she found joy in creating a cozy, smaller space that reflected her current self rather than the mother she once was.

With a softened demeanor, Harold began to share his own story. He talked about the day he and his late wife had painted their living room, the countless family gatherings, and the shared laughter in the backyard. As he spoke, he admitted that the memories kept him anchored, but he also mentioned the overwhelming upkeep and worry about the property as they aged.

Listening to each other's experiences allowed both friends to connect on a deeper level, fostering understanding and empathy. They realized that their fears stemmed from different sources. Margaret feared isolation in a large home, while Harold feared losing his cherished memories.

With this newfound understanding, they both began to consider that downsizing could be a shared experience rather than an end to their memories. Together, they explored local options for smaller homes that still allowed them to hold onto their pasts while welcoming new beginnings.

Eventually, they found a lovely senior community that offered smaller apartments along with social activities. They both made the decision to move there together, excited to share this new chapter of life while still honoring the memories of their old homes.

Their friendship deepened through this journey, proving that sharing personal experiences can bridge gaps and resolve disputes, transforming challenges into opportunities for growth and friendship.

By following these steps, you can establish and maintain an environment where open dialogue thrives, fostering collaboration and connection. Opening up these channels allows each family member to articulate their thoughts and feelings clearly, reducing the likelihood of miscommunications driving wedges between people. Creating regular opportunities for open discussion—whether through family meetings or casual conversations—can help keep everyone aligned and focused on the collective goal.

Managing the Emotional Impact of Moving

Leaving a cherished home is no small feat. It's not just about packing boxes and changing addresses; it's about processing the emotional weight of the memories and experiences that have defined your life within those walls. Recognizing these emotions is vital as they are real and completely valid. Moving out of a long-term residence can stir up feelings of nostalgia, sadness, or even anxiety. These are natural responses to change and should be acknowledged rather than suppressed. Here, we look at techniques you can apply if you are struggling to manage the emotional impact sometimes associated with moving house.

Create Rituals or Commemorations

One way to navigate the tidal wave of emotions is by creating rituals or commemorations that honor the moments shared in the home. This could be as simple as hosting a farewell gathering with close friends and family or taking some time alone to walk through each room, reflecting on what each space meant to you. One example of a ritual that honors a home you're moving out of is a "Goodbye Ceremony." Here's how you can do it:

- **Gather Sentimental Items**: Collect small mementos or photographs from your time in the home.

- **Invite Friends or Family**: Have a small gathering with close friends or family to share memories.

- **Circle of Gratitude**: Form a circle and take turns sharing your favorite memories about the home or things you are grateful for.

- **Write a Letter**: Each participant can write a letter to the home, expressing gratitude for the shelter and experiences it provided.

- **Burn or Bury the Letter**: As a symbolic gesture, you can either burn the letters and let the smoke carry your sentiments away or bury them in the backyard/garden.

- **Plant a Tree or Flowers**: Consider planting a small tree or flowers to symbolize growth and new beginnings as you move on.

- **Say Goodbye**: Conclude by saying a heartfelt goodbye to the home, acknowledging the memories and experiences shared within its walls.

This ritual allows for closure and honors the space you've cherished.

By marking these memories with intentional actions, you provide yourself an opportunity to say goodbye in a meaningful way, allowing closure and making space for new beginnings.

Redefine the Concept of "Home"

Homes are more than just physical structures; they embody the life lived within them. For many, redefining the concept of "home" becomes necessary. A home isn't confined to a particular location; instead, it encompasses future experiences and opportunities yet to come. Think of it as expanding the idea of home beyond four walls to a broader sense of belonging that comes from relationships and experiences. Embracing this perspective can transform the transition from one of loss to one of potential growth and exploration.

Leaving behind a beloved space might seem daunting, but it also brings the chance to create new memories and establish fresh connections elsewhere. You may find joy in decorating your new place, integrating objects carrying sentimental value from your past into this new environment.

Summary

Navigating the emotional terrain of moving from a home you've lived in for several years can be poignant. We've explored the importance of acknowledging these deep-seated emotions and the resistance that often accompanies change. Understanding is key—each family member may have unique attachments to their home, filled with stories and memories. By facilitating open communication and empathy, families can face these challenges with compassion and unity. Embracing active listening and collaborative decision-making helps ease tensions and ensures everyone feels included in shaping their future together.

As you embark on this significant transition, remember that it's okay to feel the weight of leaving behind something so familiar. Creating rituals to honor the past and seeking ways to redefine what "home" means can unlock new opportunities for growth and connection. Finding comfort in sentimental keepsakes and integrating them into your new space can connect old memories with new beginnings. Through clear communication, respect for differing opinions, and adaptability, families can build a supportive environment that makes embracing change just a little bit easier.

Chapter 10

Sustaining Your New Lifestyle

Sustaining your new lifestyle involves a delicate dance between intention and routine. Here, we look at those everyday strategies that help nurture your newly adopted lifestyle without feeling overwhelmed. Imagine setting small, achievable goals that integrate seamlessly into your daily habits, making them second nature. It's a matter of letting change gently weave itself into the fabric of your life until, before you know it, you're not just living differently—you're thriving.

Below, we'll look at various ways to enhance and maintain these changes so you thrive in your new home. By integrating these insights, you'll be well-equipped to carry your new lifestyle forward smoothly.

Maintaining a Clutter-Free Environment

Creating and sustaining a clutter-free environment involves developing habits that keep your space organized while maximizing peace of mind. Maintaining a clutter-free environment in small homes is important, as small homes have limited space, and keeping it clutter-free allows for better use of the available area. This helps create a more functional living environment where every item has its place. Maintaining a clutter-free environment in small homes fosters a more enjoyable, functional, and peaceful living space.

A clutter-free environment comes with considerable psychological benefits, including reduced stress and enhanced focus. Living amidst clutter can contribute to elevated cortisol levels, increasing stress and anxiety. It's common to feel overwhelmed when surrounded by too many things, as if the items themselves demand attention and care. On the contrary, an organized space allows for easier navigation and encourages mental clarity. When your home feels orderly, it fosters a sense of calm and promotes productivity. You're more likely to find what you're looking for, complete tasks efficiently, and experience a greater sense of satisfaction and accomplishment. Below, we look at strategies for maintaining a clutter-free environment long term.

Adhere to a Decluttering Schedule

At the heart of a clutter-free lifestyle is a consistent decluttering schedule, adapted to fit personal needs and spaces. Imagine setting aside time each week or month dedicated solely to reviewing and organizing your belongings.

This period could be as short as 15 minutes daily or a couple of hours monthly, depending on the level of clutter and available time. For some, tackling one room at a time may work best, while others might prefer addressing categories, such as clothing or books. Tailoring the schedule ensures that decluttering becomes a manageable, ongoing routine rather than an overwhelming task.

While establishing a decluttering schedule may seem daunting, breaking the process into smaller, achievable goals makes sustaining a clutter-free environment infinitely more approachable. Start small—perhaps by organizing a single drawer, then gradually progress to larger areas.

Celebrate these victories, however minor they may seem, as each step reinforces positive habits and contributes to a more organized home.

The Value of Regular Decluttering

Periodic evaluations of personal items help determine what remains relevant and necessary. Life changes, and so do personal tastes and needs. Revisiting your possessions regularly allows you to let go of those that no longer serve you, freeing up space both physically and mentally. Sometimes, certain items hold sentimental value but no practical purpose; in this case, consider preserving the memory through photographs or other creative means, ensuring the item doesn't contribute to physical clutter.

Regularly assessing your belongings can also be financially beneficial. Selling unwanted items online or through local consignment shops offers a way to recoup some of their initial cost, turning decluttering into a potentially profitable venture. Alternatively, donating gently used items not only aids those in need but also fosters a sense of community and social responsibility.

Incorporating decluttering into your lifestyle isn't just about reducing physical objects; it's about encouraging a mindset that prioritizes clarity and simplicity.

Developing mindful purchasing habits complements a clutter-free lifestyle. Before buying, ask whether the item adds value to your life or aligns with your current needs. This habit minimizes impulsive purchases and prevents future clutter from accumulating. Focusing on quality over quantity ensures that your possessions last longer and hold greater meaning. Introducing mindful purchasing habits into your life involves being intentional and conscious of your buying decisions. Here are some steps to help you cultivate these habits:

- **Assess Your Needs**: Before making a purchase, evaluate whether the item is a need or a want. Ask yourself if it will add value to your life.

- **Set a Budget**: Create a budget that outlines how much you can spend and stick to it. This helps control impulse buying and fosters financial awareness.

- **Practice Delayed Gratification**: Implement a waiting period before making a purchase. For example, wait 24 hours for smaller items or a week for larger ones to determine if it's truly necessary.

- **Research Before Buying**: Take the time to research products, comparing quality, price, and reviews. This helps ensure you make informed choices.

- **Evaluate Longevity**: Consider the durability and longevity of the item. Opt for high-quality products that will last longer over cheaper, short-term solutions.

- **Support Sustainable Brands**: Look for companies that prioritize ethical practices and sustainability. This promotes responsible purchasing and supports the environment.

- **Limit Exposure to Advertising**: Reduce your exposure to advertisements, which can trigger impulse buying. Unsubscribe from promotional emails and limit time on social media.

- **Create a Purchase List**: Maintain a list of items you genuinely need. Refer to this list when shopping to stay focused and avoid distractions.

- **Reflect on Past Purchases**: Regularly review your past purchases to evaluate their usefulness. This reflection can help you identify patterns and make better decisions going forward.

- **Practice Gratitude**: Cultivate a sense of gratitude for what you already have. This mindset can reduce the desire for new purchases.

- **Involve Others**: Share your mindful purchasing goals with friends or family. They can provide support and accountability, helping you stay committed.

By implementing these steps, you can develop mindful purchasing habits that promote intentionality and satisfaction in your buying choices.

Although maintaining a clutter-free home requires effort and commitment, the rewards are manifold. Enjoying a clean, organized space enhances overall well-being and creates a welcoming atmosphere for yourself and guests alike. The reduced stress and increased focus gained from such an environment translate into better productivity and healthier family dynamics. Remember, the journey to a clutter-free lifestyle is ongoing, adapting as personal circumstances change.

Adopting a Mindset of Intentional Living

Adopting a lifestyle centered around intentional living and conscious consumption can fundamentally reshape the way we experience our daily lives. Rather than drifting through life, making choices aligned with our true values and priorities allows us to lead with purpose. Intentional living involves being deliberate in our decisions, which means taking time to understand what truly matters to us. It's about aligning actions with these personal beliefs and goals, creating a coherent path reflective of who we are and who we aspire to be. Intentional living is a lifestyle choice that emphasizes making conscious decisions and taking deliberate actions to align your life with your values, goals, and purpose. It involves being aware of how you spend your time, resources, and energy, rather than allowing habits, societal expectations, or distractions to dictate your choices. Here are key aspects of intentional living:

- **Clarity of Values**: Understand your core values and principles, which guide your decisions and priorities.

- **Goal-Setting**: Establish meaningful goals that resonate with your values and vision for your life, focusing on what truly matters to you.

- **Mindfulness**: Practice being present and aware in your daily life, which helps you make thoughtful choices rather than acting on autopilot.

- **Decluttering**: Simplify your life by removing distractions, unnecessary possessions, and commitments that don't align with your intentions.

- **Focus on Quality**: Prioritize quality over quantity in relationships, experiences, and possessions, ensuring that what you have contributes positively to your life.

- **Sustainable Practices**: Embrace sustainability in your choices, considering the impact of your actions on the environment and society.

- **Intentional Relationships**: Foster relationships that uplift and support you, surrounding yourself with people who share or respect your values.

- **Financial Mindfulness**: Spend money intentionally, aligning your financial decisions with your objectives rather than succumbing to consumer habits.

- **Continuous Reflection**: Regularly evaluate your life, choices, and progress toward your goals to ensure you remain aligned with your intentions.

- **Prioritizing Well-Being**: Make choices that support your mental, emotional, and physical health, recognizing their importance in living intentionally.

By practicing intentional living, you can lead a more fulfilling and purpose-driven life, ultimately enhancing your overall well-being and happiness. We discuss some of the integral aspects of intentional living below.

Mindful Consumption

Mindful consumption is an integral part of intentional living. Mindful consumption involves being acutely aware of the environmental and ethical impacts our purchasing decisions can have. By understanding where products come from, how they are made, and their journey to us, we become more conscious consumers. This mindset shift prompts us to support brands that prioritize sustainable practices and fair trade, ensuring our purchases contribute positively to the world (Guevarra, 2023).

One of the significant challenges many face while transitioning to this mindset is overcoming impulsive buying habits. The temptation for immediate gratification is often spurred by marketing and sales tactics or emotional needs. To resist this, focus on quality over quantity. Investing in high-quality items that last longer not only reduces waste but also brings a sense of satisfaction knowing you've chosen something worthwhile. For instance, rather than buying multiple pairs of cheap shoes that wear out quickly, one might choose a durable pair made from ethically sourced materials. This not only saves money in the long run but also reduces clutter and contributes to a more sustainable lifestyle.

Making Conscious Choices

The journey to intentional living opens up the possibility of living a more meaningful and satisfying life. When you make choices consciously, they feel more rewarding because they're aligned with your inner compass, providing clarity and peace of mind. Imagine waking up every day knowing that your life reflects your values and aspirations. This alignment transforms mundane tasks into opportunities for growth and fulfillment. It's about enjoying the process as much as the outcome, finding joy in the simple, everyday moments that accumulate to form our lives.

Living intentionally often involves questioning societal norms and the "shoulds" that dictate how we live. The pressure to conform can lead us away from what genuinely makes us happy. Living with intention means defining success on our terms, whether that's having more free time, pursuing passions, or cultivating relationships. It's not about achieving perfection but embracing a continuous learning process where we refine and adapt our lives toward what's truly important (*What is intentional living*, 2024).

Practical Tips for Intentional Living

Incorporating the principles of intentional living into daily life requires patience and persistence. Start small, by reflecting on daily habits and identifying areas misaligned with your values. Gradually replace them with actions that bring joy and peace. If, for example, spending too much time on social media leaves you feeling drained, consider setting boundaries to reduce usage, allowing more room for activities that enrich your life, like reading or spending quality time with loved ones.

Another practical approach, directly related to decluttering and downsizing, involves simplifying physical spaces. A cluttered home often mirrors a cluttered mind, making it challenging to focus on what truly matters. By decluttering and organizing spaces, we create environments conducive to intentional living. Each item should serve a purpose or bring happiness, reducing distractions and promoting tranquility.

It's also beneficial to engage in regular self-reflection. This practice helps identify shifts in priorities and adjust actions accordingly. Life stages change, and so do our goals; maintaining flexibility ensures that we remain on a path that resonates with our evolving selves. Whether it's downsizing for retirement or adopting a slower pace, intentional living supports these transitions smoothly and purposefully.

Embracing Change and Evolving Your Space as Life Moves Forward

Adapting to life's constant changes can feel challenging, but proactive space evolution can offer a smoother transition. Our living spaces should evolve with us, reflecting our current needs and future aspirations. As we journey through different phases of life, our homes must remain flexible havens that accommodate these shifts seamlessly. Here, we present some tips that will help you evolve your space as life moves forward.

Make Your Home Adaptable

Life is anything but static; it's dynamic, always changing and demanding that we adapt along with it. Our homes should echo this rhythm by being as adaptable as possible. Think of your living space as a canvas that you can repaint at any stage—adding new colors that represent different parts of your life. Whether it's moving furniture around to better suit your lifestyle or adjusting layouts to create more room for new activities, embracing flexibility can make all the difference. This idea doesn't just help practically but can also breathe new life into your home—creating energy and excitement even during challenging transitions.

Personal growth often sparks a need for updating home design and organization. Imagine stepping into a chapter where you're pursuing new hobbies or taking on work-from-home roles; your home should support these shifts. Maybe it's time to carve out a nook for your painting supplies or set up a desk corner optimized for productivity. These updates are essential, as they provide the physical space necessary for personal development. The shift might require some trial and error—rearranging a few times until you find what best supports your growing needs and goals.

Furthermore, incorporating multifunctional furniture and adaptable layouts can significantly aid in accommodating life's inevitable changes. Consider investing in pieces like convertible sofas, extendable tables, or wall-mounted desks that can serve dual purposes. A guest room doesn't have to be just an occasional sanctuary for visitors; with the right setup, it can double as a home office or hobby space when needed. Movable partitions or shelves on wheels can redefine a room's purpose without permanent alterations, making adaptability not only practical but also cost effective.

Reflect and Set Clear Goals

Reflecting on personal experiences and setting clear goals play a crucial role in anticipating future adjustments. Taking time to reflect allows you to assess how well your current environment supports your lifestyle. Are there areas that feel cramped or underutilized? Are certain routines becoming cumbersome due to a lack of space or functionality? By understanding what's working and what's not, you lay the groundwork for intentional change. Establishing goals gives direction, ensuring that any adjustments made will lead to spaces that align with lifestyle aspirations. Whether you're eyeing retirement, a new job, or welcoming family additions, having clarity concerning your goals makes preparing your space much easier.

When thinking about how to continue embracing change and evolving your space as life progresses, keep a few guidelines in mind.

- Start small—change doesn't have to happen overnight.

- Tackle one area at a time, allowing yourself to adjust and understand the impact before moving on to another.

- Frequently check in with yourself or other household members to see if changes are still meeting everyone's needs. This ongoing evaluation ensures your home continues to be a place of comfort and functionality.

Summary

Embracing a clutter-free lifestyle and intentional living requires both consistency and adaptability to maintain in the long run. Here we've explored practical strategies to help maintain your newly adopted lifestyle through regular decluttering routines and mindful consumption. By integrating manageable habits, like the "one in, one out" rule, or incorporating storage solutions tailored to your needs, maintaining an organized environment becomes less daunting. These small changes make a big difference, turning decluttering into a process that benefits not just your space but also your mental clarity and overall well-being.

As you journey through life's changes, remember that your home is a reflection of yourself and should evolve as you do. Personal growth often calls for rethinking how your space supports your current lifestyle. Whether you're exploring new hobbies or adapting to working from home, your home should be flexible enough to accommodate these changes. Embrace simplicity by investing in multifunctional furniture or rearranging layouts to suit fresh needs. It's about making your environment work for you, providing comfort and functionality at every stage of life. Keep evaluating and adjusting your space to ensure it continually meets your evolving goals, creating a serene and purposeful environment that truly feels like home.

Conclusion

As you close the final chapter of this book, it's a wonderful time to pause and reflect on the profound journey you've embarked upon. Downsizing isn't just about reducing your square footage or clearing out old belongings; it's a transformative experience that affects every aspect of your life. It's an opportunity for personal growth, allowing you to embrace change, explore new possibilities, and become more attuned to what truly matters.

Throughout this book, we've explored the practical steps and emotional aspects of transitioning to a smaller space. Yet the most compelling part of this journey is witnessing how it reshapes us from within. By letting go of excess material possessions, we also let go of mental clutter. There's a newfound clarity that emerges when we're no longer weighed down by things that no longer serve us. This clarity can lead to unexpected personal growth, offering us insights into who we are and what we value.

This downsizing journey often reveals strengths we never knew we possessed: resilience, adaptability, and creativity in carving out a life that's intentionally simpler yet profoundly richer. Amid all the sorting and decision-making, you might have discovered a new sense of self, one that thrives on freedom rather than accumulation. It's not just about making do with less but reveling in the abundance of experiences, relationships, and love that fill your life.

Remember, home is not defined by its size or location but by the love and memories nestled within its walls. Whether your new abode is a quaint cottage, a chic urban apartment, or a cozy house in the suburbs, what truly makes it home is the tapestry of familial bonds, friendships, and cherished moments you weave there. As you curate this new living space, you'll find that every corner reflects who you are now—resilient, hopeful, and eager to craft new memories in this fresh chapter of life.

An Ongoing Adventure

This journey toward a simpler, more intentional life doesn't end here. It's an ongoing adventure that invites you to keep exploring ways to live authentically and joyfully. It isn't just about having less but enjoying more—more peace, more connection, and more freedom to pursue passions that bring fulfillment. As you move forward, continue to seek out experiences that resonate with your spirit and bring joy to your days.

In closing, I want to extend heartfelt encouragement to you for the road ahead. May you find beauty in the smaller spaces you inhabit, richness in a carefully curated life, and joy in each step taken toward a future crafted by choice rather than circumstance. Embrace this stage of life as a time to grow, explore, and relish the simplicity that brings you closer to the essence of who you are.

As you say goodbye to the things that once defined your past, welcome the myriad of experiences that will shape your future. Home is wherever you choose to plant your heart. Fill it with laughter, warmth, and memories. Live intentionally, guided by the values that matter most to you. You deserve a life that reflects your dreams and passions, unfettered by unnecessary baggage.

Take this leap of faith with optimism. The best is yet to come, and you are uniquely prepared to embrace it. Here's to a future filled with love, laughter, and endless opportunities to live a meaningful, fulfilling life. Welcome to your fresh start—your new chapter awaits!

References

7 tips for helping your elderly parents downsize (2024, May 1). Wellspring Center for Prevention. https://wellspringprevention.org/blog/downsizing-senior-parents-home/

9 effortless ways to improve records management (2024). Archive Corporation. https://www.archivecorp.com/ways-to-improve-records-management/

Badush, A. (2024, April 1). *What happens when you declutter?* E-ZCleanUp. https://ezcleanup.com/what-happens-when-you-declutter/

Basu, A. (2024, May 3). *Expand your living space: Top furniture solutions for space efficiency.* Artisan Furniture. https://www.artisanfurniture.net/news/expand-your-living-space-top-furniture-solutions-for-space-efficiency/

Becker, J. (2024, May 13). *10 creative ways to declutter your home.* Becoming Minimalist. https://www.becomingminimalist.com/creative-ways-to-declutter/

Casillas, J. C., Moreno-Menéndez, A. M., Barbero, J. L., and Clinton, E. (2018). Retrenchment strategies and family involvement: The role of survival risk. *Family Business Review* 32 (1). https://doi.org/10.1177/0894486518794605

Collins, D. (2022, October 27). *How big of a house do I really need?* Quicken Loans. https://www.quickenloans.com/learn/how-big-of-a-house-do-i-need

Communication skills in family therapy: Improving connection (2024). Carrus Behavioral Hospital. https://behavioral.carrushealth.com/2024/03/08/communication-skills-in-family-therapy-improving-connection/

Coping with isolation: 25 strategies for optimizing mental health (2020, April 29). St Bonaventure University Online. https://online.sbu.edu/news/coping-with-isolation

Donating goods. (2024). Charity Navigator. https://www.charitynavigator.org/donor-basics/other-ways-to-give/donating-goods/

Ellefson, L. (2024, May 10). *All the tools you need to motivate you to declutter.* Lifehacker. https://lifehacker.com/home/best-tools-to-declutter

Elgoibar, P., Ruiz-Palomino, P., and Gutierrez-Broncano, S. (2024). Laissez-faire leadership, trust in subordinates and problem-solving conflict management: A multigroup analysis across family-non-family businesses. *European Management Journal.* https://doi.org/10.1016/j.emj.2024.04.009

Family matters: How assisted living can support your loved one (2024). Bonaventure Senior Living. https://bonaventuresenior.com/family-matters-how-assisted-living-can-support-your-loved-one/

Fostering autonomy in At Home Elder Care: Empowering independence and well-being (2024, March 19). Family Resource Home Care. https://www.familyresourcehomecare.com/autonomy-at-home-elder-care/

From chaos to calm: Effective decluttering strategies (2024, July 8). Happy Housekeepers. https://happyhousekeepers.com.ph/from-chaos-to-calm-effective-decluttering-strategies/

From downsizing to rightsizing: Navigating senior life transitions with ease (2024, February 19). Sadie G. Mays. https://www.sgmays.org/senior-life-transitions/

Gordon, S. (2024, April 24). *The Connection between cleanliness and mental health: Here's why decluttering can help spark joy and boost mood.* Verywellmind. https://www.verywellmind.com/how-mental-health-and-cleaning-are-connected-5097496

Grieving a space and how grief counseling helps (2024, January 29). WOC Therapy. https://woctherapy.com/grieving-a-space-and-how-grief-counseling-helps/

Guevarra, D. (2023, April 15). *Mindful consumption: Living consciously for a better world.* The Fresh Writes. https://medium.com/thefreshwrites/mindful-consumption-living-consciously-for-a-better-world-445a1825dd4c

Hazardous waste recycling (2024, June 14). EPA: United States Environmental Protection Agency. https://www.epa.gov/hw/hazardous-waste-recycling

How to address and declutter sentimental items (2020, February 19). Rachel and Company. https://rachelrosenthal.co/2020-2-19-how-to-declutter-sentimental-items/

How to decide the ideal size of your home. (2024, June 19). Williams Homes. https://www.williamshomes.com/blog/how-to-decide-the-ideal-size-of-your-home/

How to declutter sentimental items (2024). Modern Minimalism. https://modernminimalism.com/how-to-declutter-sentimental-items/

How to donate stuff responsibly (n.d.). Ethically Kate. https://ethicallykate.com/blog/how-to-donate-stuff-responsibly

How to pack for a move: A checklist by room (n.d.). Constellation. https://www.constellation.com/energy-101/moving/moving-packing-checklist.html

How to pack for a move: Room by room checklist (2024). David McCarthy Moving. https://www.davidmccarthymoving.com/blog/10-helpful-packing-tips-for-moving/

Ingla, F. (2024). *Multifunctional spaces: What are they are how to optimize space?* Pedra. https://pedra.so/blog/multifunctional-spaces

Innovative and effective solutions for recycling: Reducing waste and maximizing impact (2024, October 16). Happen Ventures. https://happenventures.com/innovative-and-effective-solutions-for-recycling-reducing-waste-and-maximizing-impact/

Introduction to flexible living: A new era of living (2024, March 6). Coliving.com. https://coliving.com/blog/introduction-to-flexible-living-a-new-era-of-housing

Knyszewski, J. (2024, August 12). *Embracing minimalism: How simplifying your life can lead to greater happiness and efficiency.* Medium. https://medium.com/@thejeromeknyszewski/embracing-minimalism-how-simplifying-your-life-can-lead-to-greater-happiness-and-efficiency-ea16d90e7c97

Lawson, A. (2022, October 24). *Marie Kondo and the KonMari method: The ultimate guide.* Abby Organizes. https://justagirlandherblog.com/marie-kondo-konmari-method/

Lawson, A. (2023, January 6). *How to get organized when you live in a small house.* Abby Organizes. https://justagirlandherblog.com/how-to-get-organized-when-you-live-in-a-small-house/

Leader, G. (2023, December 21). *Embrace simplified living and a minimalist simplified life with simple living.* Task Slayerz. https://www.taskslayerz.com/simplified-living/

Luborsky, M. R., Lysack, C. L., and Van Nuil, J. (2011). Refashioning one's place in time: Stories of household downsizing in later life. *Journal of Aging Studies* 25 (3): 243-252. https://doi.org/10.1016/j.jaging.2011.03.009

Macnaghten, C. (2024, October 10). *Benefits of downsizing for a simpler life.* Cooling Off Period. https://coolingoffperiod.com.au/benefits-of-downsizing-for-a-simpler-life/

Madeson, M. (2023, December 19). *23 family therapy techniques to strengthen your relationships.* PositivePsychology.com. https://positivepsychology.com/family-therapy-techniques/

Maletic, M. (2024, February 12). *20 under-the-bed storage ideas to efficiently maximize your space*. Elegance Echoes. https://eleganceechoes.com/under-the-bed-storage/

Matthews, M. (2023, December 9). *Embracing change: Navigating the ups and downs of downsizing for seniors*. Medium. https://medium.com/@arbormove/embracing-change-navigating-the-ups-and-downs-of-downsizing-for-seniors-72b6a1991bcb

MESHDS (2024, June 6). *Guide to effective document management and archiving*. MES Hybrid Document Systems. https://blog.mesltd.ca/guide-to-effective-document-management-and-archiving

Miller, D. (2023, December 4). *Efficient college storage: A guide to organizing your dorm space*. Storage Scholars. https://www.storagescholars.com/blog/efficient-college-storage-a-guide-to-organizing-your-dorm-space

Peter, (2024, June 23). *Strategies for enhancing family dynamics in MFT*. TherapyPM. https://therapypms.com/dealing-with-complicated-family-dynamic-cases-try-these-strategies/

Ruth, (2023, December 21). *Moving home with kids and pets*. A Swift Move. https://aswiftmove.co.uk/moving-home-with-kids-and-pets/

Schroeder-Gardner, M. (2023, September 20). *How I flip garage sale items on eBay as a side hustle*. Making Sense of Cents. https://www.makingsenseofcents.com/2021/04/how-i-flip-garage-sale-items-on-ebay.html

Sen, E.A. (2023, October 29). *The role of flexible interiors in modern living*. Illustrarch. https://illustrarch.com/articles/18505-the-role-of-flexible-interiors-in-modern-living.html

Shaw, N. (2024). *Embracing minimalism: The art and benefits of decluttering*. Lifehack. https://vocal.media/lifehack/embracing-minimalism-the-art-and-benefits-of-decluttering

Spring organizing using color coding labels (2024, April 3). InStockLabels.com. https://instocklabels.com/blog/organizing-with-color-coding-labels/

The best ways to sell your stuff. (2014, August). Consumer Reports. https://www.consumerreports.org/cro/magazine/2014/09/the-best-ways-to-sell-your-stuff/index.htm

The joy of paperless post and party planning (2019, March 8). Life Organized. https://www.life-organized.com/category/digital-decluttering/

The ultimate guide to mastering the art of labeling and sorting your items (2024). Koova. https://koova.com/blogs/news/the-ultimate-guide-to-mastering-the-art-of-labeling-and-sorting-your-items?

Tips for creating a cozy & inviting home - make your living space warm & welcoming. (2024). Zerorez Carpet Cleaning. https://www.zerorez.com/blog/tips-for-creating-a-cozy-inviting-home-make-your-living-space-warm-welcoming

Varghese, M., Kirpekar, V., and Loganathan, S. (2020). Family interventions: Basic principles and techniques. *Indian Journal of Psychiatry* 62 (2): 192-200. https://doi.org/10.4103/psychiatry.indianjpsychiatry_770_19

Verduyn, M. (n.d.). *Organizational restructuring: 7 strategies for HR (plus free template).* AIHR. https://www.aihr.com/blog/organizational-restructuring/

What are the three pillars of strategic planning: Building a solid foundation for success. (2024). Quantive. https://quantive.com/resources/articles/what-are-the-three-pillars-of-strategic-planning

What is intentional living? (2024, October 28). Balance Through Simplicity. https://balancethroughsimplicity.com/how-to-live-with-intention-this-year/

What is the KonMari method? (2024). KonMari. https://konmari.com/about-the-konmari-method/

What not to do when downsizing? (2024, July 9). LifeCycle Transitions https://lifecycletransitions.com/what-not-to-do-when-downsizing/

Williams, C. (2024, March 4). *Moving locally with kids: A complete guide for a stress-free relocation.* Alien Movers. https://www.alienmover.com/moving-locally-with-kids

Image References

Cameron, J.M. (2021, January 26). *Woman with dreadlocks and man in yellow t-shirt sorting clothes standing next to each other.* Pexels. https://www.pexels.com/photo/woman-with-dreadlocks-and-man-in-yellow-t-shirt-sorting-clothes-standing-next-to-each-other-6994855/

Cottonbro studio. (2020, May 22). *Inside kitchen apartment box.* Pexels. https://www.pexels.com/photo/inside-kitchen-apartment-box-4569323/

Cottonbro studio. (2021, February 24). *Women packing their things.* Pexels. https://www.pexels.com/photo/women-packing-their-things-6942741/

Kaboompics.com. (2021, January 31). *A woman in white shirt holding clear glass jar.* Pexels. https://www.pexels.com/photo/a-woman-in-white-shirt-holding-clear-glass-jar-6660254/

Kaboompics.com. (2020, May 28). *Glad woman writing down notes during while packing.* Pexels. https://www.pexels.com/photo/glad-woman-writing-down-notes-during-while-packing-4506226/

Lach, R. (2021, April 29). *Woman in gray and black shirt standing beside brown wooden table.* Pexels. https://www.pexels.com/photo/woman-in-gray-and-black-shirt-standing-beside-brown-wooden-table-8285738/

Mart Production. (2021, March 30). Man and woman standing by the door. Pexels. https://www.pexels.com/photo/man-and-woman-standing-by-the-door-7329679/

Piacquadio, A. (2019, March 5). *Concentrated woman carrying stack of cardboard boxes for relocation.* Pexels. https://www.pexels.com/photo/concentrated-woman-carrying-stack-of-cardboard-boxes-for-relocation-3791617/

RDNE Stock project. (2021, July 1). *Assortment of items on carton boxes.* Pexels. https://www.pexels.com/photo/assortment-of-items-on-carton-boxes-8581372/

Subiyanto, K. (2020, April 26). Pleasant woman preparing stuff for moving. Pexels. https://www.pexels.com/photo/pleasant-woman-preparing-stuff-for-moving-4247756/

About the Author

Rebecca Lawson is a leading expert in the field of home organization and decluttering, celebrated for her ability to transform overwhelming spaces into harmonious, intentional environments. With years of hands-on experience guiding individuals and families through the often emotional and practical challenges of downsizing, Rebecca has established herself as a compassionate and knowledgeable advocate for simpler, more fulfilling living. Her book, *Decluttering and Downsizing the Family Home: Strategies for a Stress-Free Transition,* serves as a comprehensive guide, equipping readers with actionable strategies to reduce clutter, preserve cherished memories, and embrace the freedom of a more manageable lifestyle.

Rebecca's expertise extends beyond mere organization; she understands the deeply personal and emotional journey that accompanies the decision to downsize. Drawing from her own experiences and countless success stories, she approaches each situation with empathy, offering practical tools and techniques to help individuals make confident decisions about what to keep, what to let go, and how to create spaces that reflect their values and aspirations.

Rebecca is passionate about inspiring others to reimagine their relationships with their belongings and take meaningful steps toward a less cluttered, more purposeful life. She believes that by simplifying our physical spaces, we create room for personal growth, deeper connections, and the freedom to focus on what truly matters. When she's not helping others on their decluttering journeys, Rebecca enjoys exploring minimalist design, hiking in nature, and creating lasting memories with her own family.

About the Publisher

At JMcG Press, we are passionate about storytelling and ideas that inspire, inform, and entertain. As an independent publisher, we embrace diverse voices and genres, curating books that spark curiosity and create meaningful connections with readers. From thought-provoking non-fiction to immersive fiction and everything in between, our mission is to bring fresh perspectives to the page and to the world.

Your support means everything to us! If you've enjoyed one of our books, please consider leaving a review. Your feedback not only helps our authors thrive but also empowers small publishers like us to continue championing creativity and unique stories. Thank you for being part of our journey!